Writing Appalachia: One Year of Essays

Joshua Wilkey

Copyright © 2018 Joshua Wilkey
All rights reserved.
ISBN: 1986904326
ISBN-13: 978-1986904322

This is for all the folks who give a damn about Appalachia and the people who live here.

CONTENTS

	Introduction	4
1	What/Where/Who is Appalachia?	6
2	Blessed are the White Trash	12
3	Distilling Poverty in Coal Country	18
4	My Mother Wasn't Trash	25
5	Being Poor Ain't Cheap	34
6	Big Pharma Profits From Our Heartbreak	41
7	You Are Not An Imposter	54
8	Poverty, Privilege, and Dead American Dream	59
9	My Mother's Keeper	65
10	Ticonderoga Pencils and Poverty	76
11	Surprised by Trump's Popularity in Appalachia?	80
12	Appalachia Needs a Reformation	89
13	The White-Trashification of the Opioid Epidemic	101
14	Today, On Lockdown, I Didn't Miss My Gun	109
15	I Don't Write About Crafts	117

ACKNOWLEDGMENTS

While I know that my wife Betsy is my biggest fan, her mother Katie, my mother-in-law, gives her a challenge for the title. Without regular affirmation from Betsy, Katie, and Dave Aspinwall, I doubt I would have ever found the courage to tell my story in such a vulnerable and public way.

As you'll learn from the essays that follow, I have not always had a wonderful family life. However, when I married Betsy, I hit the in-laws lottery. Their unending support, love, and encouragement means more than words can ever describe. It has sustained me on this journey from historian to writer to activist.

WRITING APPALACHIA

Introduction

This project began one morning on the drive in to work. At a stoplight, I glanced down at my phone and noticed the renewal notification for my website, www.thisappalachialife.com. It occurred to me that I had been writing essays for the website for nearly a year, and I thought it might be fun to assemble the most popular essays for an edited collection as a way to mark the first anniversary of the website. So here we are.

In many ways, this has been a banner year for Appalachian writers. Largely in response to J. D. Vance's book *Hillbilly Elegy*, a number of new books and essays have emerged to challenge troublesome stereotypes. While I have researched and written about Appalachia for a number of years, Vance's book was one of the primary motivators in me beginning to write for public rather than academic audiences.

I hope that the essays presented here offer a nuanced and complicated view of Appalachia, because if you put down this book believing you understand the region completely, I might have failed as a writer. None of us are able to understand all of Appalachia, and viewing it through a single frame isn't enough. If we zoom out too far, we are subject to generalizations that are inaccurate, offensive, and dangerous. When we zoom in too far, though, we miss the region's incredible diversity.

Appalachia is neither monolithic nor static. By the time these words make it from my fingertips to your eyes, Appalachia will have changed again. Only through understanding the region in deep historical, cultural, and political context can we interpret and find meaning in Appalachia without reducing the region and its people to caricatures. It is my hope that the essays here will point you toward a better understanding of the issues that dominate the region even if I leave you with more questions than answers.

I don't like linear narratives, especially when it comes to Appalachia. We have been preconditioned by the bullshit version of history we learned as kids to believe that stories about America demonstrate continuous progress. This doesn't match what really happened in American history, and it damned sure doesn't work when telling the real history of Appalachia. As a result, my essays – and, by extension, this book – are presented in ways that reject linear and progressive narratives in favor of truth. Ugly, messy truth. If you read something about Appalachia that doesn't break your heart and piss you off, then it has probably been glossed over in some way. I hope this book peels back the false veneer so often plastered on the region in order to reveal the hurt, the pain, the hope, and the humanity present in this place.

The essays that follow are mostly in their original form, as published on This Appalachia Life, though I have made a few edits for clarification or to address issues of chronology. I have included the date of original publication for each essay in order to help readers understand them in proper context. They are presented here in the order in which they were written. The final essay, "I Don't Write About Crafts," is new, and will appear only in this book and not on the blog.

What/Where/Who is Appalachia?

April 27, 2017

This essay was one of the first pieces I published on This Appalachia Life. To understand Appalachia, one must first understand how the region is defined, both by those in the region and those outside. What follows is my best effort at defining Appalachia.

Appalachia is a place. It is defined on maps, even when competing mapmakers disagree about its boundaries. It is also a culture, even though that culture is not uniform in nature across the region.

For generations, America's most talented writers have understood the power and importance of place in the human psyche. Imagine Faulkner's work set in the midwest, or Steinbeck's work set in New England. It just doesn't work. Place matters in the telling of any decent story. In Appalachia, place matters as much, arguably, as any other factor. We can define place both as geography and as landscape. That is, lines on a map, and geological and ecological features that characterize the space inside those lines. However, in endeavoring to define Appalachia, one quickly realizes that there exists no hard, fast, and universal definition.

A logical starting point for defining Appalachia might be the Appalachian Regional Commission. At the time of this writing, the ARC still exists, though if President Trump has his way, the Commission will soon be scrapped. Established in 1965, the ARC's mission is to improve the economy of Appalachia. In order to work toward that mission, of course, the Commission by necessity must define Appalachia. That, it turns out, is often as much about politics as about culture or geography.

The ARC map, which can be found rather easily on their website, offers a quick glimpse at the bizarre outcome that results from politicians attempting to define a region. Because the ARC is able to offer federal money in the form of workforce development, infrastructure improvement grants, and community development, it has been, at times, desirable for communities to define themselves as being in Appalachia even if they do not quite seem to fit the mold. If one were to ask what any of the 420 counties in white has in common with every one of the other 419, the answer might be that inclusion in the ARC's definition of Appalachia is the only common characteristic. The map includes some parts of the deep South that are most assuredly not Appalachia. Muscle Shoals, Alabama is, technically at least, in Appalachia. The University of Mississippi is only a few miles removed from the border. There's also that tiny sliver of middle Tennessee, and part of bourbon country in central Kentucky, both of which look like random appendages and have no mountains. When one considers the driving factors behind the map, one might conclude that the ARC's definition is not, after all, a solid representation of where Appalachia really is.

Even if the ARC's map includes places that are decidedly not Appalachia, the region, as defined by the Commission, does include a very large chunk of land that is most assuredly Appalachia. That is, there are no places in the blue part of the map that are Appalachia, even if there are pieces of the white that are not Appalachia. This conundrum, then, leads us to consider other ways of defining Appalachia. While geography is certainly one important way to define Appalachia, culture and economy also factor in.

When one thinks of Appalachian culture, one might think of the noble mountaineer or the less noble white-trash hillbilly. As offensive as hillbilly stereotypes are, they remain the default when many Americans think of Appalachia. Even if they cannot point to the region on a map, many Americans are certain that hillbillies marry their siblings, live in shacks, shoot all of their food, make illicit whiskey, and remain uneducated. Sometimes, when folks from outside the region come to visit, they find tourist meccas like Gatlinburg and Pigeon Forge that reinforce these idiotic and unrealistic stereotypes.

Looking beyond offensive stereotypes, it becomes clear that there exists no single, monolithic Appalachian culture. The region cannot even be defined by race. While a goodly portion of the residents of Appalachia can trace their ancestry back to Scots Irish settlers, this is not always the case. In many communities in western North Carolina, there has existed for generations a multi-racial society. In Jackson County, where I live, for instance, one will find the Eastern Band of Cherokee Indians. Alongside whites and the Cherokees, there is a small but thriving black community. Many families in our community count as ancestors individuals of all three races. There are, I am certain, many other places in Appalachia that are not as lily-white as might be expected.

It has also been long assumed by popular culture that Appalachia, particularly the central and southern parts of the region, identifies with mainstream southern culture. This, too, is an assumption that has little root in historical reality. While there are certainly parts of Appalachia that are both southern and in the South, not all Appalachians are, or have traditionally been, Confederate-flag-flying good ol' boys. East Tennessee, for example, a region that is thoroughly Appalachian, was a hotbed of Union sympathy during the Civil War. The rebel flags that adorn porches and pickup trucks across Appalachia are generally new additions with little historical precedent. The folks flying the stars and bars today in much of Appalachia would likely be shocked that their great-great-great grandparents were Unionists through and through. However,

Americans have rarely met a stereotype they didn't latch onto, and the result is yet another flawed way to define Appalachia.

Appalachian folks are both isolated and independent, too, right? Actually, the historical record does not support the argument that Appalachia is isolated. The region was a major gateway to the American West. Coal from central Appalachia has powered the world for over a century. Timber from the region was used to build structures in much of the rest of the country. Mountain folks have long been connected to the outside world even if they chose to moderate the amount of influence the outside world has on their culture. The idea that Appalachian people are independent, too, crumbles upon close scrutiny. In many of the most impoverished parts of the region, dependence (both on neighbors and government assistance) has become necessary. Seldom where there ever fully independent mountaineers.

What, then, is authentic Appalachian culture? Does such a thing even exist? What say you?

If you are still reading, I hope you are more confused than ever about what or where or who Appalachia is. I tell my students every semester that my goal is for them to leave my class knowing less about history than when they began. This happens by virtue of them realizing just how much they do not know, and how much of what they think they know is utter nonsense. Let's face it: especially in today's social-media-driven society, many Americans are not interested in complex narratives. They'd rather have simply talking-point-worthy answers to complex questions. Hence the oversimplified explanations of Appalachia.

Now that we have established the problematic nature of using maps and culture to define Appalachia, we can examine one final lens through which to view and potentially define Appalachia. If nothing else, Appalachia is characterized by poverty. In fact, it was the region's stark poverty that drove federal elected officials to create the ARC. In 1965, after visiting some of the region's poorest communities, President

Lyndon Johnson declared an unconditional war on poverty, describing Appalachia as ground zero in that war.

Johnson remarked: "In our history no region has contributed more to the shaping of our destiny." Of course, this statement is problematic for a number of reasons. Johnson was a pretty blatant racist, and it's worth questioning his motives in finding noble white folks to rescue in the midst of the nationwide push for civil rights for African Americans. However, even though I'm not certain he fully understood the historical context, he is right that Appalachia has contributed much to the development of the United States. Unfortunately, the United States has never fully compensated the people of the region for all they sacrificed for the benefit of increased wealth in other regions.

Not all of Appalachia is poor, and many Appalachian people are poor in ways that do not fit the typical mold of poverty. There are pockets of affluence in the region, and the region's resources have been exploited to generate a great deal of wealth even when that wealth did not stay in the region. In short, there is not one single economic reality for the whole of the region. However, even if the poverty isn't the same throughout the region, and even if some parts of Appalachia have thrived economically, it is no less true that Appalachia is a region in economic distress. In fact, it is poverty and economic distress, more than any other factor, that drives the bizarre ARC map.

Examining *why* so much of Appalachia is mired in poverty is not the same as simply describing the extent of the poverty. My own scholarly work focuses on *why* much more than *what*. However, before we can dive too deeply into causation, we must first define Appalachia, or, at least, determine that no universal definition exists.

Just as Appalachia is not particularly a monolithic place, not all Appalachian people are alike. My wife and and I grow and preserve vegetables in part because of our desire for fresh and responsible food, but also because of my deep ancestral connections to the land. We fight for social justice and advocate for and end to poverty because we are driven to do so by our faith, but also because we care deeply about our neighbors. Until we begin to view each other as humans rather than as anonymous others, we stand little chance of solving the important problems of our region.

When Johnson signed the "Appalachia Bill" that established the ARC, he argued: "This legislation marks the end of an era of partisan cynicism towards human want and misery." We now know that that partisan cynicism returned with a vengeance, assuming it ever in fact fully departed. Too often, our struggling neighbors are derided as lazy, addicted, ignorant welfare cheats. When we demonize their character rather than work to understand the roots of their suffering, we are being selfish and hateful. If anything, perhaps, Appalachian people are characterized by a deep commitment to community. I hope we can all, red and blue, right and left, draw on that historical commitment to community as we continue to work toward solving the important problems facing our region.

JOSHUA WILKEY

Blessed are the White Trash

May 5, 2017

While I didn't create This Appalachia Life as an outlet for my scholarly work, I soon realized that there existed a genuine need for critical and thoughtful analysis of Appalachia. I wrote this essay as a way of defining my own relationship with the region, particularly as that relationship intersects with my professional identity as an historian and educator. What follows is a call to action for those who write about the region. It is also the essay that launched This Appalachia Life wider than I could have ever imagined.

I grew up poor.

Often, when one reads memoirs or oral histories from folks who grew up where I did -- that is, in Appalachia, or in the South, or somewhere that's either both or in-between -- one will see a disclaimer from the speaker or writer indicating that while they were poor, they didn't know it at the time. That is, though they were poor by the numbers, their basic needs were met, and they were surrounded by others facing similar economic realities. For me, that was not the case. I was poor, and I knew it. We had substantially less than most folks in our community, and I knew that too. My mother had a less glamorous and lower-paying job than did the parents of most of my classmates, and I knew it. Sometimes, we'd move on short notice because we couldn't pay the rent. Sometimes, the move was a temporary or extended stay with family members. We ate a lot of boxed macaroni and cheese, we consumed plenty of cheap hot dogs, and steaks were a tax return treat. We lived in an assortment of rented trailers for much of my childhood, a fact that made me unbearably self-conscious. In short, as I said, I knew we were poor. I knew that most folks around us considered us to be white trash. I also knew, in the way children know something they can't articulate, that I would probably be poor all my life.

Today, despite the odds, I'm not poor. My wife and I live a comfortable middle-class life. We aren't rich, and sometimes we still worry about money, but our direct payroll deposits at the end of the month keep coming, staving off any crisis, real or imagined. Our cars aren't new, but they are nice. Our home isn't huge, but it's a hell of a lot nicer than any of the homes I occupied growing up. I still eat mac and cheese, but only by choice. These days, we prefer organic veggies, whether homegrown or store-bought. I have a master's degree and I'm working toward a doctorate. My wife already has a doctorate. She's a psychologist, and I'm a college professor and writer. Sometimes, for me, social media is a stark reminder that very few of the poor people I grew up with were able to escape the twisted and life-strangling web of poverty in which we were mired growing up. It turns out that I am one of the lucky ones. I am the statistical anomaly, and I think about this almost every day of my life.

Earlier this week, as some of my students were furiously writing their final exam essays, I happened to run **across a recent essay by David Joy, published by "The Bitter Southerner."** Though I have never met him, he and I grew up in the same county, finished both undergrad and graduate degrees at the same university, and I'm told, share a mutual love for Innovation Brewing. Joy's essay cut straight to my soul. He articulated so many of the things I had felt all my life but rarely admitted. There's a sort of raw truth in his words that reveals something important about Appalachia.

Joy writes: "I'm tired of an America where all the folks I've ever loved are dismissed as trash, where people are reduced to something subhuman simply because of where they live. I'm tired of having to explain it. I'm just goddamn tired."

Those words brought the tears to my eyes. I, too, am tired of seeing the people I love - MY people - reduced to lazy, ignorant hillbillies. I'm tired of seeing them labeled as trailer trash who face the burdens they carry through some vague or unarticulated fault of their own making. I'm ready for Americans to take a long, hard look at why Appalachia is the way it is; I want people to begin to think critically about the plight of poor people, not just in Appalachia but in all of America, in historical context.

I have spent a goodly portion of my life since entering academia attempting to explain Appalachian poverty. At first, I thought that perhaps I lacked the credibility to write about Appalachia because I grew up here. Later, I thought that I could write about the region so long as I did not inject my own story into my work. Now, I realize, I have a responsibility to write about my region and my people specifically because I have experienced the heartbreaking realities of Appalachian poverty firsthand, first as a child growing up poor in the mountains, and later, as an observer who sees the tragedies and realities firsthand almost every day of my life.

In central Appalachia's coal country, where I lived for seven years of my adult life, people are often poor because of coal and not in spite of it. Similarly, in southern Appalachia people are often poor because of tourism rather than in spite of it. When one seriously considers the history of the region, particularly the economic history, one realizes that Appalachia is a rich land with poor people.

I remember being caught off guard the first time I heard Appalachia described in that way, as "a rich land with poor people." I was in my first semester of graduate school, already in my mid-thirties, and I had lived my whole life here without thoughtfully considering the stark contrast between the region's abundant natural resources and the people who had never experienced anything resembling abundance.

When poor Appalachian people are reduced to being white trash, it seems, in a rather twisted way, more reasonable that their resources can be exploited and extracted without adequate compensation. When hardworking men and women in central Appalachia are portrayed as dumb hillbillies, it is easier to pretend that coal companies are benevolent saviors rather than plunderers treating the region as a sort of internal colony. It seems more plausible, when Appalachian people are stripped of their humanity, that they should be sent down mine shafts to break their bodies and their hearts for the benefit out-of-town coal barons making a mint on the backs of the working poor, while such exploitation is heralded as a boostraps-up opportunity. When a new Chevrolet and a double-wide counts as making it big in a region marked by stark poverty, it is easier to pretend that coal jobs are a step up rather than a crushing boot to the throat. When a region is tagged a "Big White Ghetto," it is easier to destroy its environment, rip off its mountaintops, and poison its water for profit.

As revealed in the previous essay, there exists no single story of Appalachia, nor of Appalachian poverty. Not all of Appalachia is in coal country. However, tourism, timber, or iron can be inserted in the place of coal to make a rather convincing case that in most of Appalachia both poor people and their land have been exploited for the benefit of those who have no desire to live here. From hardwood flooring to cheap electricity to affordable vacations and second homes, much of the rest of the Eastern United States benefits from the sacrifices made by those who call these mountains their home.

Many of the people I grew up with, and many of my family members, are stuck in an impoverishing system that they do not understand. They do not understand it, frankly, because they do not have the time to think about it. Joy writes: "It's hard to be hopeful when you're worried about your next meal, when the only thought to ever cross your mind is how you're going to make it through the day." So, too, is it hard for folks to consider the cause of their station in life when they are worried about important things like paying the rent and feeding their kids their next meal.

The goal of my scholarly work has become translating academic jargon and theory about poverty and Appalachia into a language that might reach average Americans who know no more about Appalachia than what they see on the news or in reality television. It is difficult at best to understand the complex historical, economic, and sociological forces that lead people like my mother to end up living their lives as white trash, looked down on by those who are interested neither in the academic explanations nor the humans behind the circumstances. My mother lived all 55 years of her life, I think, knowing that she came from nothing and was destined to have nothing. She died mired in the same poverty in which she spent most of her life. I can assure you, this was not her choice. And I can assure you that I am the exception, not the rule, because I became upwardly mobile.

Many of us who write and teach about Appalachia come from a background of poverty or white trash, though few of us are quick to admit it. For those of us with roots here, our work is sometimes an attempt to understand our upbringings and sometimes an attempt to help others see the world around us as we have seen it. For most of us, it is more than a form of therapy. It is a form of action. As I continue to write about the region that is my home, and the region's impoverished people who are more like me than most of my colleagues will ever realize, I hope to find the words that might make people start giving a damn.

We MUST write about and study the problems of Appalachia, and we must learn to do so in ways that reach beyond our own isolated academic circles. We have to find meaningful ways to engage the public at large with our work and with what Joy describes as "a landscape drenched with humanity." Until we are successful in injecting that unvarnished humanity into our scholarly work, in a way that is more narrative-driven and less theoretical, we stand little chance of getting average Americans to look beyond the cruel stereotypes and heartbreaking statistics. But writing about it alone is not enough. We must allow our work to change us, and we must hope that it changes our readers, too.

    Blessed are the white trash, for they are humans too.

Distilling Poverty in Coal Country

May 8, 2017

One of the most difficult parts of writing about Appalachia is debunking commonly-held myths, especially those held by Appalachian people. In many parts of the region, coal remains king, even though it has never contributed as much to the region as it has taken. This analysis offers a critical look at the numbers behind the coal industry.

In Appalachia, our biggest export is people.

I have heard that all my life. I continue to hear it from small-town politicians concerned about brain drain. I hear it from economic development officials concerned that the steady stream of young folks leaving town makes it difficult to attract new employers. I hear it from heartbroken parents and grandparents who want their children to build lives in the region but understand that there's nothing here that gives their kids any hope for a brighter future.

The result, many argue, is that the best and brightest and socioeconomically mobile leave town while those who are too poor to move simply stay.

Among the most popular myths about Appalachia is that coal has been a blessing and a wealth-builder for the region. The previous eight years brought an overwhelming amount of rhetoric from Republican local, state, and federal officials who represent coal country. Time and again, folks in the coalfields were warned about President Obama's so-called war on coal. The EPA, people were told, was trying to kill Appalachia. Critical analysis of the numbers, however, tells a much different story. Obama didn't kill coal. Technology and market forces did.

Politicians can use statistics the way Jim Bakker uses the Bible: to argue any possible point, no matter how false or ridiculous. It was Mark Twain who popularized the oft-quoted rebuttal to statistics. There are lies, damned lies, and statistics, he quipped. While this might be true, numbers are still an invaluable way to analyze and understand both the past and the present. As an historian, I understand the necessity of building a contextual framework around numbers. When left to stand for themselves, statistics are more easily fudged or misinterpreted or downright misrepresented. In coal country, the numbers can only be understood in historical context over a long length of time.

Much of my own research is centered in the coalfields of eastern Kentucky. I lived there for seven years before I became an academic, and I learned many important lessons about Appalachia's poverty and economy in my time running a small business there. The coalfields offer an interesting and compelling example of how numbers often disprove political rhetoric.

The current consensus story of the coal economy as told by many eastern Kentucky political figures goes something like this: Coal companies have, for decades, been benevolent saviors of the communities in which they operate. They have provided high-paying jobs and opportunities for people with few other opportunities. Then Obama was elected and declared war on coal, leaving Appalachian communities to suffer and starve. Because of Obama, the story goes, eastern Kentucky damned near died. When Donald Trump began campaigning in the region, he promised a return of King Coal. If he were elected, he promised, tens of thousands of Appalachian coal miners would be put back to work.

While this storyline continues to fill those in coal country with false hope and get politicians elected, it is nonsense. Coal began its tumble well before Obama was elected. Coal employment in eastern Kentucky has been falling since the Reagan administration, even during coal booms where production soared. The numbers prove that this is the case.

In 1980, eastern Kentucky's coalfields produced approximately 109,000,000 short tons of coal with a workforce of 34,500. A decade later, in 1990, the region yielded over 128,000,000 short tons of coal with fewer than 25,000 workers. That's an increase of 17% in production, with a workforce that was almost 28% smaller. Ten years later, in 2000, production had fallen to 105,000,000 short tons, but employment fell below 13,000 workers. By 2010, production was down to 68,000,000 short tons, while employment had risen slightly to nearly 14,000.

Two things stand out here. First, as production rose in the 1980s, employment fell. Second, as production fell in the 2000s, employment remained nearly constant. These numbers debunk the myth that Obama alone was responsible for the decline of coal jobs in Appalachia.

Between 1980 and 2000, coal jobs in eastern Kentucky declined by 62%. By looking at changes over the course of three decades, it is easier to see long-term trends that are not as evident in a year-by-year analysis. Coal employment fell during both Republican and Democratic administrations, and these changes were not tied directly to changes in coal production. Changes in technology, machinery, and technique, more than changes in federal policy, led to the substantial decrease in coal employment and the increase in production. Once mountaintop removal became widespread, coal companies were able to extract more coal and they were able to do it with less labor. The result: fewer miners running coal and exponentially increased profits for the coal operators.

In 1990, the average price of a short ton of coal was $21.76 ($41.64 in 2017 inflation-adjusted dollars). That means that, in 2017 dollars, $5,346,409,440 in coal was extracted from eastern Kentucky in 1990. While they extracted billions of dollars worth of coal, coal companies simultaneously figured out how to do it cheaper. In the process, they put thousands of miners out of work. Those looking to assign blame for the decline of coal jobs in eastern Kentucky need to look back a lot farther than Obama. While he and congressional liberals might make convenient scapegoats, they are less to blame than the coal companies looking to make increased profits with fewer employees.

As coal employment fell in eastern Kentucky, so did the population in many of the most productive coal counties. Twelve of the 32 coal-producing counties in eastern Kentucky saw a decline in population between 1960 and 2010. Those that lost the most residents were generally those that produced the most coal. Even when production was booming in the 1980s and 1990s, poverty was on the rise. In 1980, a quarter of the population of the eastern Kentucky coalfields lived below the poverty line. By 1990, that figure had risen to thirty percent. That is, even as coal production increased, so did poverty rates. By 2000, the poverty level had declined a bit to 26%, but only because the population had increased slightly across the region, mostly in counties like Laurel, which is located on the interstate and less dependent on coal. In fact, Laurel County alone accounts for over half of the population growth in the region between 1990 and 2000. Counties that relied more heavily on coal did not fare so well.

Of the twelve counties that had a smaller population in 2010 than in 1960, only three of them are no longer major coal producers. Harlan County is a glaring example of a county in crisis. Harlan lost 44% of its population in the half-century between 1960 and 2010. This is despite the fact that coal companies extracted tens of millions of dollars worth of coal from Harlan County in the same span of time. If a booming coal industry drove the eastern Kentucky economy in the way many would have us believe, why was Harlan's population shrinking while its coal industry was booming? The simple answer is that coal operators were employing fewer miners. Those who could afford to do so simply left town to find other opportunities.

A declining population in eastern Kentucky presents a unique problem. When the national economy was booming, as it was in the 1990s, those who were laid off from coal jobs and unable to find other work stood a better chance of finding jobs in other places. However, as the economy began a not-so-subtle meltdown in 2007, it became less likely that those unable to find work in the region had the resources or the opportunity to move. For generations, Americans have "voted with their feet" by moving to other places when they were unable to find work. However, in eastern Kentucky, when fewer and fewer people have the resources to move, only those who are at least somewhat financially stable or upwardly mobile are able to leave. As the population shrinks, those who leave are often the more-mobile middle class. The result is that the shrinking population is increasingly made up of poor people. I call this process the distillation of poverty.

Let's look at a hypothetical example to demonstrate how the math works. A hypothetical county with a population of 10,000 has a poverty rate of 25%. That's 2,500 impoverished people. Let's say the county's population decreases by ten percent, and only those above the poverty line are able to afford the move. That leaves a population of 9,000, but there are still 2,500 impoverished people in the county. The poverty level then rises to 27.7%.

Harlan County offers an example of this process at work. In 1980, the poverty rate in Harlan was 25.8%. By 1990, it increased to 33.1%. During the same time period, the population decreased by over 5,000 people. The result is that in 1990, impoverished people made up a larger percentage of the population. This process plays out in many eastern Kentucky counties in the 1980s, 1990s, and 2000s. When poor people make up an increasing percentage of a given county's population, it becomes an ever greater challenge to offer the services (education and job training, namely) necessary to help these individuals escape from poverty.

In 2010, 26.3% of the population in eastern Kentucky lived below the poverty line. At the same time, only 15% of all Americans were impoverished. When one out of every four people in a given region lives in poverty, it is a challenge for political and business leaders to create and foster opportunity for those who seek it. Impoverished people are less likely to be healthy, and they are afforded fewer educational opportunities. Accordingly, they stand a diminished chance compared to most Americans to climb out of poverty, no matter how hard they work. Employers are put off by counties with high poverty rates for a variety of reasons. Right or wrong, they buy into the idea that high poverty rates mean an unqualified and untrained workforce. This perpetuates many of the inaccurate and hurtful stereotypes about Appalachian people. Without education and job training, and without new employers to replace coal jobs, poverty becomes permanent. Eventually, people assume that those who rely on public assistance to survive are just lazy.

It has at times (including this time) been popular to blame poor people for their circumstances rather than blaming the broken system that prevents them from achieving upward mobility. JD Vance's recent bestseller *Hillbilly Elegy* treads this insulting path. Vance is heavy on victim blaming, and many reviewers have **called him out for it**. I see it all the time, particularly on social media. Those who have never experienced soul-crushing poverty themselves insult and belittle those who are forced to survive on public assistance. They label them "white trash" and "hillbillies." They rob them of their humanity. They blame them for being poor as if they somehow had a choice. They preach about accountability and personal responsibility while never holding those who have systemically exploited Appalachia accountable for the plundering they have been doing for generations.

I say often that central Appalachia is poor because of coal rather than in spite of it. After first writing this in my essay titled "Blessed are the White Trash," I got a bit of pushback via social media. A few folks accused me of being anti-coal, and more than one person expressed displeasure at what I said "about coal miners." To be clear, I am quite anti-coal, but I am very pro-coal-miner. I believe coal is the single worst thing to have ever happened to white people in Appalachia. I believe that many coal operators are evil. I believe that any person who runs a company that makes profit from poisoning water and destroying mountains should be ashamed. I believe that coal operators who have hired gun thugs to intimidate and threaten and beat coal miners should be arrested and tried and thrown under the jail.

I also believe that coal miners should be fairly compensated for their work. They take risks that are not usually worth the rewards, and their sacrifices have powered and built America and the world for generations. They should be supported and taken care of when their bodies are broken by their work, especially when their injuries are due to unsafe working conditions. I believe they should be free to unionize and bargain collectively without threats from mine operators. In short, I believe they should be treated like humans rather than like expendable and replaceable pieces of equipment.

As we continue to debate the future of coal in the United States, we must put aside the political rhetoric. We must look to the past to determine what led us to here. We must consider a future for the coalfields that does not include coal, because no matter what legislative or administrative changes Congress or President Trump push through, the market and technology have spoken and determined that coal miners are on their way out even if coal remains. This process was set in motion decades ago, and few people, including **coal operators themselves**, believe there will be a resurgence in coal jobs in Appalachia. I hope we can all find ways to engage in dialogue about the role the coal industry has played in creating and fostering poverty in the region. In the process, I hope we can avoid victim-blaming and stop dehumanizing people who have had no choice but to simply survive in poverty.

My Mother Wasn't Trash

May 10, 2017

If "Blessed are the White Trash" is the essay that launched This Appalachia Life higher than I ever imagined possible, this is the essay that solidified my calling as an activist and as a voice for those in Appalachia who remain unheard. While the essay that follows is my own writing, it is also a reflection of the collective heartbreaking sentiment of a region of hurting people. Incidentally, I stand by my assertion that certain conservative political figures mentioned herein are assholes.

My mother died the day she turned 55.

This Sunday will be my first Mother's Day without her, but nearly a year after she died, I still find it impossible to be heartbroken over her passing. As I wrote in her obituary, she suffered from both mental and physical illness for much of her life. However, despite her struggles, she selflessly loved and supported those who meant the most to her. In so many ways, she loved those who society deemed outcast and unloveable, and through her relentless love of others, her relationship with God was readily apparent. While I miss her dearly, it would be selfish of me to wish that she were still alive and suffering rather than at peace.

I suppose that my mother is the single biggest reason that I have devoted much of my career to studying poverty. My mother was what some folks call white trash, and by extension, that made me white trash growing up too. Truth is, she never stood much of a chance of climbing out of the poverty in which she became mired the minute she was born. Her father was an alcoholic and her mother was (and still is) about as wicked a human as I have ever met. Mom and her sister mostly raised themselves, so it's no wonder they got married and left their abusive home first chance they got. At 16, Mom married an alcoholic who beat her most every day until the night he came home drunk and she rolled him up in the bedsheets and beat the hell out of him with a baseball bat. Not long after, she got pregnant. Her firstborn child died before he was a week old. She named him Dustin David, and his loss laid heavy on her heart for the rest of her life. It was just one piece of a lifetime of heartbreaking burden that took a toll on her mental health.

Not long after Dusty died, she met my father and my conception hastened the bells of Mom's second wedding. My father is a good man, but they divorced by the time I was out of diapers. After my father, she married a total of five more times, twice to the same man. She had the biggest heart of anyone I have ever known, but picking men was not among her gifts. She told me more than once that she didn't think she deserved a good man. I was never able to convince her that she deserved a partner who treated her well.

Mom didn't finish high school, but she decided to pursue an education when I was a kid. She found it harder and harder to make ends meet working as a gas station attendant and grocery store cashier, and education seemed like a good solution. She earned a GED, then a diploma from a technical college. Nobody in her family had ever finished high school, much less attended tech school, and I will never forget how proud of her I was when I saw her walk across the stage and get her diploma. I was in middle school at the time, but I vowed that someday I would go to a tech school and maybe even get a four-year degree because I wanted her to be as proud of me as I was of her in that moment. For poor people, occasions for pride are so few and far between. Sense of accomplishment is a pleasure rarely afforded to those who are impoverished. I suppose that is why I still choke up every time someone I love tells me they are proud of me. The truth is, Mom would have been proud of me no matter what.

As hard as she worked, Mom was never able to fully escape poverty. Even after she became qualified to work in an office rather than behind a cash register, she remained a part of what economists call the working poor. It turns out that all those years of lifting and standing while working dead-end jobs had taken a toll on her body. By the time she finally landed an office job with benefits, she needed lower back surgery. For the last twenty years of her life, she lived with chronic pain, and she tried an endless array of prescription drugs - both those prescribed to her and those not - but she never could keep the pain at bay.

Three years before she died, husband number six threw her to the ground and choked her until she nearly blacked out, then forced her to watch as he put a bullet in his heart. She never recovered emotionally, but somehow she found the capacity for love again. Just months before her own death, she married a final time when a man she had recently fallen in love with was diagnosed with terminal cancer and given less than a month to live. His last wish was that she would accept his marriage proposal, and she obliged.

Because of a lifetime of poverty or a lifetime of mental and physical abuse or some combination of the two, Mom's mental health began to deteriorate by the time she reached forty. She suffered from anxiety and depression and bipolar disorder. On at least six occasions, she attempted suicide. Twice, I had to initiate involuntary commitment because she refused to seek the inpatient psychiatric care she so deeply needed.

She buried two husbands in less than two years, decades after having buried her firstborn. So many of the people in her life that she should have been able to rely on for love and support over the course of her lifetime betrayed her through abuse and neglect. I am convinced that she died of a broken heart even though the coroner said she died from an abscess in her lung. For weeks after she died, I felt guilty because I felt relieved. However, the night she died was the first night in years that I was able to fall asleep without worrying about whether or not Mom was safe.

At first reading, the story of my mother's life seems like little more than a tragedy. However, it is much more than that. Her story reveals the stark realities of growing up poor. All across Appalachia, there are thousands of women just like my mother working, striving, struggling, just to exist. So many people in Appalachia have broken minds and broken bodies and broken hearts, and they do nothing more than survive because that's all they can do.

It is as popular now as ever to blame poor people for their station in life. Republican politicians love to talk about how poor people could stop being poor if only they made better choices or worked harder. **If only they'd stop buying iPhones, they could afford insurance!** These assholes - and I do not use that slur lightly - have no clue what it is like to grow up poor. They have no clue how hard it is in many places in the US just to keep the lights on and food on the table. It is easy for them, from the comfort of their cushy offices and homes, with full bellies and bank accounts, to pretend that poor people like my mother are poor because they are stupid or lazy or ignorant or irresponsible rather than confront the broken systems that perpetuate poverty in Appalachia and all across the US. Poor people don't contribute to reelection funds, but those who profit from poor people sure do. Therefore, truth be told, most politicians couldn't care less about the plight of the poor. There's so much profit to be made from poor people - think payday loans, high-interest rent-to-own stores, for-profit colleges, and overpriced mobile homes - that politicians and their crony-capitalist donors have a vested interest in keeping them poor.

Many of us who have personal experience with poverty understand that addiction, mental illness, poor health, and lack of education are symptoms of poverty rather than causes. When I think about all the suffering my mother endured over the course of her life, I can't help but wonder how anyone could think that she was to blame for her poverty. She started working at 12, and she worked every day for years, long after her body gave out on her. She made choices, some good, and plenty bad, but poor people have fewer options when faced with impending and potentially life-changing decisions. Poor people like Mom are often forced to choose from a small number of shitty options, and most of them try to find the one that is slightly less shitty than the others. When people are eaten up mentally and physically by a lifetime of compounded shitty choices, they reach a point where they can't even decide what is best anymore, because they realize that no matter what they do - no matter how hard they try - they are cogs in a broken machine and nobody cares about them anyway. Poor Appalachian people are broken, but not nearly as broken as the systems that keep them poor.

In the days since I posted a blog entry titled "Blessed are the White Trash," my website has been visited by over 35,000 unique users. The link has been shared over 500 times on Facebook, just counting the shares I know about. Over 100 new people have connected with me via social media, and I get dozens of emails every day from folks reaching out to share their stories and let me know that my own story resonates with them.[1] I started this blog as a means of reorienting my own writing style away from academic jargon and back toward narrative-driven language aimed at general audiences. I didn't imagine anyone would read it other than my wife and a few friends. However, I struck a nerve, it seems. The overwhelming response is not at all a testament to anything I have done, but rather, a clear indication that people just need to know that they matter and that somebody gives a damn about them and their stories, especially if they are poor.

David Joy, who is by my estimation the most talented and important young writer in Appalachia right now, **recently wrote**: "The

---

[1] Since writing this essay, my website has attracted over 1,000,000 visitors, and I have lost count of all the other statistics. In short: It's a hell of a lot more people than I ever imagined would read anything I wrote.

truth is we live in a world where we don't listen to people anymore. So often we're just waiting for the next opening to respond. What we need to realize is that sometimes people don't need advice. Sometimes people just need to be heard. Sometimes the greatest gift we can give someone is just to keep our mouths shut and let them empty themselves into our hands. When they're finished, we don't need to do anything with what they've given us. We just need to show them that we're holding it for them till they can catch their breath."

Sometimes, that's all Mom needed. Someone to be present while she screamed and cried. Somebody to hold her while she caught her breath. Somebody who would listen to her problems rather than tell her how she ought to solve them. I am ashamed to admit that, particularly after I reached adulthood and found financial stability, I was more interested in trying to fix her problems than in listening to her tell me about them. When I finally began climbing out of the murky bog of poverty, I thought I could just hand her a fifty dollar bill or pay her car insurance and make things a little better for her. Surely, I thought, helping her out financially would be useful and meaningful. Looking back, I realize that, like most poor people in Appalachia, giving a damn to her meant listening and loving, not fixing. Like so many people in her situation, she was robbed of her voice for her entire life. Nobody wanted to listen.

Judging from the emails I have received in the past few days, a good many people are interested in the way their own communities and stories are playing out right now to a national audience. They realize that people are listening, it seems, but are unsure that their voices are actually being heard. At least a fourth of the folks who have reached out since I published "Blessed are the White Trash" have asked how I feel about J. D. Vance's bestselling book *Hillbilly Elegy*. This book has, for many Americans, become their primary source of information about Appalachian culture and poverty. The short answer is that I disagree with both Vance's conclusions and his methodology. As I told a group of my students recently, I am heartbroken that *Hillbilly Elegy* will likely be the most popular and important book about Appalachia in a generation.

Vance writes: "I don't know what the answer is, precisely, but I know it starts when we stop blaming Obama or Bush or faceless companies and ask ourselves what we can do to make things better" (256). While this is not blatant victim-blaming, it comes close. This line of reasoning promotes the individualistic philosophy so prominent among those on the political right in the US. It sounds like it came directly from the pen of Ayn Rand. It calls for a bootstraps-up set of solutions for people who lack boots. It calls on poor people to fix their own problems by changing their culture. Vance calls it a "culture in crisis." What his book lacks, however, is the important historical and economic context that explains how Appalachia came to be impoverished. While he is critical of Appalachian culture, he doesn't bother to find out how it came to be as it is.

For generations, first with timber and coal and later with tourism, Appalachia has served as a sort of internal colony for the rest of the United States. People with no desire to live here came to pillage and plunder. They cheated Appalachian people out of their land and their resources, their dignity and their humanity. In central Appalachia, coal companies engaged in ruthless and ethically bankrupt tactics like using the broad form deed. They moved people into coal camps where they paid them poorly and forced them to buy everything from the overpriced company store. They were compelled to work and remain silent or become homeless. In southern Appalachia, timber barons came for the lumber. They clear-cut the mountains and left environmental and economic devastation in their wake. In both instances, Appalachian people were transformed from independent farmers and craftspeople into laborers treated like nothing more than replaceable parts. They were deprived of their resources, and the profit most certainly didn't flow back into their communities. Today, all that remains in much of Appalachia are minimum wage service jobs. In the more touristy parts of the region, the people whose ancestors once thrived in these mountains now serve sweet tea and fried chicken to the vacationing descendants of those whose communities and wealth were built in part with the resources extracted from Appalachia.

In the United States, our approach to solving Appalachian poverty doesn't differ substantially from our approach to solving African poverty. In both cases, outsiders came in to exploit resources and left generations of poverty in their wake. While the process was substantially more extreme, racist, and violent in Africa, in both cases conservative political leaders think those left behind economically should just make better decisions and stop being poor. That approach will not work in either instance. Neither will sending food and secondhand clothing. And don't even get me started on the idiotic and theologically-flawed thinking that leads fundamentalist Christians to think they can solve poverty by evangelizing the poor folk.

While we must not approach any instance of poverty, whether in Kinshasa, Congo or Frakes, Kentucky, with the flawed notion that we fully understand it, we must understand that the solutions will be found in action both by those who are impoverished and by those who are not. This is not a problem to be fixed by condescending outsiders, but neither is it a problem to be fixed only by those who are impoverished. Neither group can fix it alone.

The process starts, I think, with taking time to listen. Then, we can try to understand. I might understand it a little better than most because I grew up white trash. I have seen my mother and my family members and my neighbors be forced to make impossible choices between a limited number of shitty options. I have at times had to make those impossible choices myself. Even having grown up poor and having spent my academic career researching and writing about poverty, I do not claim to understand it fully. We must realize that there exists no single narrative about Appalachian poverty. Not all poor people are the same. Not all impoverished families fit into a single category even if they are united by similar demographics.

When my mother died, she had fifty-six cents in her bank account. Had someone told her they really needed that fifty-six cents, she would have given it to them without a second thought. She lived in a world that led her to understand the importance - no, the necessity - of helping others. If there's any hope at all for fixing the brokenness in Appalachia, it lies with those who have a servant's heart. It starts with putting aside condescending and selfish beliefs. It starts with taking a lesson from my sweet little mama and loving the outcast and the unloveable.

It starts with listening instead of talking.

JOSHUA WILKEY

Being Poor Ain't Cheap

May 16, 2017

This essay was inspired by a trip to the dollar store one summer afternoon. I needed to swap out a propane tank, and when I was paying, I was reminded that many retailers who serve the poorest members of our communities prey on the impoverished with idiotic fees that most of the rest of us are fortunate to avoid. I stewed all the way home, and after I swapped out the propane, finished the burgers, and took a heartburn pill, this essay emerged before bedtime.

Poor people are cash cows.

It makes no sense, really. One would think that poor people, by virtue of being poor, would not be profitable customers. However, for many large corporations that target the poor and working poor, there's big money to be made on the backs of those who have no money.

At Dollar General Store locations, customers can get cash back on their purchases. This is not novel. In fact, most all retailers these days offer this option. Soccer moms get cash back so they can have lunch money for their children. Restaurant patrons can get money back to leave a cash tip for their servers. I sometimes get cash back at the grocery store so I can buy Girl Scouts cookies on the way out. It's a simple process. Click "yes" when the little screen asks for cash back, tap the $20 icon, and the cashier hands you some bucks along with your receipt. We've all done it. For those who are poor and those of us who are not but who have limited retail options, however, there's often a sinister catch.

I noticed this a few years ago, first at Dollar Tree, then at Dollar General. There's a little asterisk after the standard "would you like cash back?" prompt. The footnote indicates that "a transaction fee may apply." The transaction fee is usually $1 no matter the amount of cash back. If one opts to get $10 cash back, one is charged a dollar. That's a ten percent fee, for a service that costs the retailer nothing. It's just another way for retailers like Dollar General to make a profit off of their customers, many of whom are very often living below the poverty line.

If an organic grocer or movie theater were charging a fee of this sort, I would likely be annoyed by it, but I wouldn't be so annoyed that I would write about it. However, the poorest members of our communities do not shop at Whole Foods, and they do not often get a chance to go see the latest blockbuster at the theater. They can afford neither. In fact, they likely do not have either organic grocers or first-run theaters in their neighborhoods. Instead, they have Dollar General. Dollar General's stores grow like kudzo in rural America. Even if there isn't a real grocery store in most tiny communities, there's probably a DG.

These ridiculous transaction fees are but one example of how corporations make billions of dollars by taking advantage of socioeconomically disadvantaged customers with few options. There are many other examples, though, and politicians continue to allow it at the expense of their poorest and most marginalized constituents.

Payday lending is one of the most sinister ways that large corporations exploit poor people. For those who are not familiar, payday lending goes something like this: People who are running short on money but who have a verified record of regular income (whether it be Social Security, SSI, payroll, etc.) are able to go to payday lenders and receive a cash loan to be repaid on payday. Often, borrowers are unable to repay their full loan balances and simply "roll over" their loan until a future payday, accruing all sorts of fees and additional interest. The annualized interest rate on these loans is often in the triple digits. Yes, that's right. Sometimes the annual interest rate is over one hundred percent.

In defense of this practice, many payday lenders and their high-dollar lobbyists argue that they are simply offering a service to poor borrowers that said borrowers cannot obtain anywhere else. This is partially true. The poorest members of society have no access to traditional forms of credit. Some even lack access to checking accounts because of low credit scores or a history of financial missteps.

I know some people who make occasional use of payday lending because they genuinely have emergencies arise that they could not address without a short-term infusion of cash. I also know people, including members of my own family, who have been riding the high-interest payday loan merry-go-round for years, and who have paid thousands more back than they have borrowed yet still owe more. In debating the role of payday lending in our communities, it is essential that we take a nuanced approach. Some form of short-term credit is necessary for those mired in poverty. However, it is flat-out immoral that we regulate payday lending so loosely in many places that people end up feeling crushed under the weight of small high-interest loans that they have no hope of ever repaying. Taking out a $1,000 payday loan should not mean a person **becomes tied to tens of thousands of dollars in debt.**

Another egregious example of corporations exploiting the poor is rent-to-own retailing. Companies like Aaron's and Rent-a-Center purport to offer a valuable service for the poor. Because those at the bottom of the socioeconomic spectrum are seldom able to save for big-ticket items like appliances or furniture, these retailers offer a pay-by-the-month scheme that often requires no credit check and no money down. The result is that customers pay as much as three times the retail price of the item, assuming they are able to make payments until the item is paid for. When they are not able to maintain the payments, the retailers simply show up to repossess the items.

Like payday lenders, rent-to-own retailers argue that they provide a valuable service to poor consumers. However, many observers, myself included, conclude that some rent-to-own practices are ethically questionable and tend to target vulnerable consumers who need immediate access to essentials like appliances and bedding. In many states, companies are not required to disclose the final price of the items. Instead, they simply tell customers the amount of the monthly or weekly payments. Because companies call the arrangement "rent-to-own," in many places they are not required to disclose the amount of "interest" customers will pay because it technically isn't interest. When consumers can no longer afford the payments and have to return the item, they often get no credit for payments they have made even if they have paid substantially more than the item is worth. Many customers never realize that they are paying as much as three times the retail price for their items. Those who do realize it likely have no choice apart from going without a bed or refrigerator.

In some instances, state attorneys general have successfully sued major rent-to-own retailers for violating usury and consumer protection laws. However, because these retailers are covered generally by state laws rather than by federal laws, there exists a hit-and-miss patchwork of regulations. Some consumers enjoy greater protections than others. The only determining factor is their location. Those states with more corporation-friendly attorneys general are unlikely to see any activity that might force retailers to behave more ethically toward their customers, because such enforcements will result in a drop in profitability for the retailers. Many major corporations spend good money to be sure that politicians protect their interests rather than the interests of consumers. Rent-to-own retailers and payday lenders are no exception. The poor, of course, can't afford lobbyists or political contributions.

There are some who will argue that the free market, not the federal government, is the best solution to corporations that exploit the poor. However, those at the bottom of the socioeconomic spectrum, especially the rural poor, do not live in anything resembling a free market. Also, it is important that we label the behavior of rent-to-own companies and payday lenders as what it is: exploitation.

In the hills of Appalachia, poverty is often the rule rather than the exception. One of the most poverty-stricken ZIP codes in the United States is Manchester, Kentucky. Manchester is located in Clay County, which has a population of just over 20,000 people. According to the most recent US Census data available, the per-capita income average between 2011 and 2015 was just $13,802 (less than half the national average) and 46% of the population lives below the poverty line. In Manchester, Rent-a-Center is often the go-to option for poor people looking to buy appliances or furniture. The county has a Walmart, but the nearest discount appliance and furniture dealers are miles away, too far for many to drive. There are some locally-owned options, but few in Clay County are able to pay cash for major purchases given the high rate of poverty and the low rate of employment.

In addition to the rent-to-own retailers, Clay County also has no less than five payday lenders, but only two traditional banks. Conveniently, the primary shopping center in Manchester currently houses a Dollar General, a Rent-a-Center, and two payday lending branches, all within feet of one another.

In places like Manchester, rent-to-own and payday lending outfits thrive. They do so often to the detriment of the poor folks who frequent their businesses. Those promoting the so-called free market approach might argue that customers are not forced to do business with these types of companies. However, given their dire financial circumstances and lack of available options, poor people in Manchester have little choice. They are excluded from participating in the wider world of commerce, often because of forces beyond their own control.

Manchester is not a rare exception. Particularly in central Appalachia, rent-to-own retailers are often the only option for poor people, and payday lenders outnumber banks by large measure. In addition to being food deserts, many poverty-stricken communities are retail deserts. In the most isolated rural areas in Appalachia, Dollar General is one of the only available retail options. Within ten miles of our house in rural Jackson County, NC, there are four Dollar General stores, and our community isn't even particularly isolated. Dollar General is the closest store to our home, and my wife and I tend to shop there by default because it is either that or a ten minute drive to the closest grocery store, or worse, a twenty minute drive into town. While we have the resources to go to town any time we want, many of our neighbors do not. The folks in the trailer park down the road often walk to Dollar General because they have few other options. This does not seem much like a free market driven by competition. Therefore, "free market" solutions simply do not work here.

Dollar General is, I believe, fully aware of the demographics of their shoppers. They know that there are often few ATMs near their locations, and their customers often lack access to traditional banking anyway and end up paying fees of three or four dollars to access their money at ATMs. Especially for people who depend on Social Security or SSI for their income, access to money is an important issue. Dollar General and similar retailers, it seems, understand this. Their solution is not to offer a resource for their customers but to profit from their customers' limited access to funds. It's cheaper than an ATM, but it's a fee more affluent shoppers never have to think about. While there is nothing illegal about this, it is certainly morally questionable.

That's the thing about the so-called free market. It makes no accounting for moral right or wrong. That, free market proponents allege, is up to the consumers. Poor consumers, however, still need to eat. They still need ovens and beds. Consumer choice and self-advocacy is often, like so many forms of social or political action, a full-stomach endeavor. When one is hungry, one's ability to be an activist is diminished. When poor people have no choice but to do business with the greedy companies who reap a hefty profit from their customers' lack of options, those drawing the short straw simply do what they must to survive. Surviving is what poor people do best, and it makes for a miserable life. I know, because I have been there.

When poor people have little option but to do business with discount retailers who charge cash-back fees, rent-to-own retailers who charge inflated prices, and payday lenders who mire their customers neck-deep in impossible-to-pay-back high-interest loans, they are even less likely to ever escape poverty. The stark reality is that poor people often pay substantially more for essentials – bedding, appliances, housing – than would those of us with means. If my wife and I needed a new washer, we'd shop around for the best deal and go buy it. In fact, we might even buy it from Amazon Prime and get free two-day shipping. When my mother, who lived her entire life in poverty, needed a new washer, she was forced to buy one from a rent-to-own outfit that charged her an outrageous delivery fee and hassled her every time she was even a few hours late on a payment. She probably ended up paying $2,000 for a $450 washer. The poor do not have access to Amazon Prime like the rest of us because they can't afford a hundred bucks a year to subscribe. They do not get free delivery and obscenely low prices. They get fleeced.

The limited options available to those in poverty are rarely considered by the political ideologues who are so prone to victim-blaming. These retailers, who are all too often protected by state and federal lawmakers from both parties, package their predatory tactics as opportunities. What they are really selling are tickets on yet another segment of the poverty train. The politicians who protect them should be deprived of options and see just how much more expensive it is to survive. They should be ashamed for protecting those who profit from poverty, and those of us who know about it and have the resources to fight back should be ashamed for letting it happen to our neighbors.

Big Pharma Profits From Our Heartbreak

May 30, 2017

It is essentially impossible to live in Appalachia and not see the impact of the opioid crisis in your daily life. It is written in the pages of local newspapers and visible at gas station parking lots and pawnshops all over rural America. This essay was an effort at combining my own experiences with a scholarly exploration of the problem. This essay has served as the basis for a number of speeches I have made in the region this year.

My grandmother is a drug addict.

She still refuses to admit it even though most everyone around her knows that her dependence on opioid painkillers drives nearly every part of her life. At first glance, she might look like a typical little gray-haired lady, but she lies, she cons, and she uses others in ways most of us couldn't fathom just to get the money to buy more Vicodin.

At this point, most all her family is estranged, and I am not certain she really cares. For her, the only priority is the pills. It has been this way for at least twenty years, and I'm not sure if the drug abuse made her selfish and hateful, or if she was that way before the drugs. I suspect the former. I want to believe the former. I probably need to believe the former.

As much as I would like to help her, the hard truth is that it has proven nearly impossible for any of us who are related to her to try to help her without being pulled into miserable situations ourselves. I don't know what the answer is, because I know that even as hateful and selfish as she is, she didn't choose to be a drug addict. Circumstances beyond her control dealt her a life so terrible that she came to think of drugs as the only solution. As much as I want to be angry at her, I know in my heart that she is suffering in ways I cannot begin to understand. And frankly, I consider myself blessed, lucky, whatever you want to call it, that I cannot understand myself what she is going through.

While it might seem rare, or even a bit of a novelty, for an elderly lady to be a drug addict, it really isn't that unusual in Appalachia. Addicts come in all ages here in the mountains. They come from rich families and from poor families. Addiction in Appalachia is not limited by race or by education level. It afflicts the Baptists and the Methodists and the Pentecostals and the agnostics. If you live in Appalachia, you almost certainly know someone who is, or was, an addict. In fact, you most likely know someone who died as a result of their addiction.

While addiction reaches both the rich and the poor in Appalachia, the stark reality is that addiction thrives in these mountains in large part because of poverty. The poverty came first. The drug addiction came later, often as a desperate response. The poor are disproportionally destroyed by addiction. They have the least access to treatment options, and they are more likely to escape addiction through death than through recovery. Most remain addicted all their lives, and their lives are usually cut tragically short.

Over the past few years, the opioid epidemic that is plaguing rural America has finally begun to get a bit of national attention. The evening news shows **have run a few specials, and some documentary filmmakers have made important films about the crisis.**

Today, prescription opioids have largely taken the place of heroin, methamphetamine, and crack cocaine in bringing heartache and desperation to Appalachia. These opioids don't come across the southern border or from a clandestine lab or even from a trailer park chemist. They come from multi-national corporations. They are prescribed by physicians, and purchased and dispensed, at least initially, from licensed pharmacies. The most popular form is called Oxycodone. You might know it by one of its brand names: OxyContin, Roxycodone, or Percocet. A closely-related drug, hydrocodone, is sold under brand names including Vicodin, Lorcet, and Norco. In much of Appalachia, these drugs, all of which are opioids, are household names.

While many Americans encounter these drugs only while recovering from a surgical procedure, OxyContin and other prescription opioids are responsible for thousands of deaths per year in Appalachia. According for the Centers for Disease Control, more than a thousand people per day seek treatment in US emergency rooms because they have misused prescription opioids. In 2014, the most recent year for which statistics are available, over 2,000,000 people in the United States either abused or were dependent on prescription opioids.

It all sounds so clinical and official, really, when we talk about "prescription opioids" and data compiled by the CDC. The reality, however, is that many people who abuse opioids in Appalachia buy them illegally, and getting a fix isn't cheap. In many parts of Appalachia, especially in eastern Kentucky and in West Virginia, a sort of illicit economy has developed around the widespread abuse of opioids. While the pills are manufactured by multi-national companies, prescribed by health practitioners, and dispensed by pharmacies, those to whom they are prescribed often sell them illegally. In most parts of Appalachia, street-level dealers, some of whom are addicts themselves and sell pills to support their habits, are able to get more than a dollar per milligram for the pills. A thirty milligram OxyContin, for example, will usually fetch $30. For addicts in advanced stages of addiction, a single 30 mg pill is barely enough to stave off withdrawal symptoms. It takes substantially more than that for them to get high.

Those who buy these prescription opioids illegally rarely take them in the ways intended by the manufacturers. While some addicts simply take the pills orally, many eventually end up crushing the pills and snorting them or, worse, shooting them up intravenously. It is a mind-boggling journey, really, from the tightly controlled manufacturing laboratory of a major pharmaceutical manufacturer to the vein of an addict in central Appalachia, via what might be a secondhand needle. No matter how the OxyContin gets to its final destination, however, its initial sale is still added into the black side of the manufacturer's balance sheet. As Appalachia is slowly rotted from the inside by this dangerous poison, drug company executives and shareholders are making billions.

I have always wondered: do they know? Do they care? When Mark Timney, CEO of Purdue Pharma, the maker of OxyContin, sees his direct payroll deposit hit his bank account, does he think about the hundreds of people who die every year because of his product? Does Timney think about the moral implications of running a company that makes a product that has destroyed lives and homes and towns? I suspect that Timney doesn't think about the unfortunate and hopelessly addicted end-users of his products any more than the CEO of Raytheon thinks about the collateral damage on the receiving end of the Tomahawk Missiles his company manufactures. Perhaps the world would be a better place if these aloof and isolated executives were forced to step outside their bubbles and see the gut-wrenching destruction their products cause.

If Timney had to walk through the alley behind Cumberland Avenue in Middlesboro, Kentucky and see the dirty needles lining the gutter, he might be forced to consider his moral obligations to folks other than his board or Purdue's stockholders. If he had to ride along with police officers who have to remove malnourished babies from the homes of parents who have died from OxyContin overdoses, perhaps he would understand the full implications of what he willfully does for a living. He has a choice. Those who become addicted to his product are deprived of choices by the chemistry Purdue Pharma has worked so hard to perfect.

For those of us who have seen opioids destroy families and communities and lives, it isn't much of a stretch to equate the CEO of a big pharma corporation with the CEO of a weapons maker. In the parts of

Appalachia most destroyed by prescription opiates, it sure feels like a war is happening around us even if there are few gunshots and no bombs. I have lived in a community where OxyContin has drained away hope and life and dignity. I have served as foreperson of a grand jury that indicted hundreds of drug traffickers who served as middlemen between Purdue Pharma and addicts. I have witnessed the hopeless desperation of drug addicts, including members of my own family, who would do anything – anything – for another pill.

In so many parts of Appalachia, prescription opioids are as much a part of the landscape as the mountains that surround us. I lived in Middlesboro, Kentucky, for seven years of my adult life. Even having grown up around a grandmother who has for years been on a slow march toward the grave via Vicodin, I was stunned by how much a part of the local culture prescription opioids were in eastern Kentucky.

I moved to Middlesboro in 2004, just as the meth epidemic was beginning to be addressed with tougher restrictions on the sale of precursor ingredients. As meth ebbed, OxyContin became the drug of choice.

In those days, it was easy to get. Local drug traffickers would pack busses and vans full of people from the hollers and hills. They'd head down I-75 to Florida where unscrupulous health practitioners would, with a wink and a nod, diagnose patients they'd never see again with chronic pain and give them a prescription for whatever opioid cocktail they'd like. Upon request, they would even throw in prescriptions for the popular sedative Xanax for good measure. The scripts could be conveniently filled by the on-premises pharmacy. The addicts would hop back on the bus and head back to Kentucky. They'd give half their pills to the drug dealer who organized the trip, as payment for the ride and the office visit charges, and keep half for themselves.

At the time, Florida lacked a statewide tracking system for prescription drugs. The same addicts could make weekly trips to different parts of Florida for month-long supplies of pills. They could have a dozen active prescriptions for OxyContin or other powerful opiates, and absent a statewide tracking system, no one in any official capacity would catch the duplication.

On more than one occasion, authorities in Kentucky caught drug traffickers with thousands of high-powered opiate painkillers in just-filled prescription bottles and were not even able to arrest them. Even though consuming just a fraction of the total number of pills prescribed per day would have killed the drug traffickers, every single pill was lawfully prescribed to the person in possession of the pills, so law enforcement in Kentucky couldn't charge them because they had not technically broken the law. The officers knew the pills would be on the streets in hours and in the veins of addicts minutes after they were sold, but the officers had no recourse.

By 2010, the problem had become so severe that some elected officials from Kentucky were lobbying their counterparts in Florida to adopt a computerized prescription drug-tracking database. However, Florida governor Rick Scott fought against the implementation of such a system citing privacy concerns and opposed funding it even though the Florida legislature approved it. Scott even went so far as to turn down a $1,000,000 contribution from Purdue Pharma to fund the database. Finally, in 2011, after pressure from members of Congress and the Obama administration, Scott relented and **approved a database.**

Even with tightened restrictions on opioid prescriptions and better monitoring databases, the problems persist in much of Appalachia. The solutions, it seems, are slow in coming. I have written previously that lawmakers often turn a blind eye while their contributors systematically exploit the poor for profit. I note that while payday lenders and rent-to-own retailers have plenty of money for lobbyists and political contributions, the poor often can't even get their congressional representatives to pick up the phone. The result is that lawmakers often tailor their rhetoric to put the blame on the drug addicts themselves rather than the companies that supply the drugs. Even the prescription tracking databases focus on finding patients breaking the law rather than on addressing the root sources of the pills. These politicians talk a whole lot about the importance of eliminating drugs from their communities, but they rarely mention the companies that created the products to begin with and spent millions of marketing dollars getting them into the hands of the people who became addicted to them.

Congress could get high-powered opiates off the streets in short order if they had the guts to do it. I might be jaded or naïve, but it seems like it would be straightforward to stop the abuse of powerful narcotics made by legitimate manufacturers. They operate from clean state-of-the-art facilities and skyscrapers, not from makeshift labs hidden in trailer parks or South American jungles. Perhaps because of the legitimacy of their businesses, the companies that make opioids seem to have more political and social cover even though their products destroy communities in the same way that meth and heroin do.

With prescription drugs, most politicians are clearly in the corner of drug companies despite their lofty rhetoric. In the healthcare debates unfolding around the United States now, many point out that drug prices in the US are substantially higher than in other developed nations. Congress, it seems, is hesitant to clamp down on drug manufacturers, and perhaps it is for good reason. In the same way that many in Congress are not willing to regulate prescription prices, they are also often unwilling to consider dramatic changes in public policy that would put a dent in the legal opioid business because such solutions would hurt the bottom lines of their corporate donors.

It's no wonder that elected representatives, even those with constituents dying every day from opioid overdoses, might think twice before taking action to cut off the flow of OxyContin to Appalachia. Big Pharma spends a lot of money to buy influence both in Congress and in state legislatures. Cartel leaders who smuggle crack or heroin can't pay congressional representatives to turn a blind eye, but through campaign contributions and lobbyists, pharmaceutical companies can.

In North Carolina, Kentucky, Tennessee, and West Virginia, the states whose mountainous regions make up the core of the Appalachian territory most hurt by opioids, pharmaceutical manufacturers have given nearly $2,000,000 in political contributions to federal-level elected officials over the past decade. From 1986 to present, these drug companies have given over five million dollars to state-level officials and candidates for state legislative seats. $7,000,000 has flowed directly from drug companies to elected officials while thousands of dead bodies are left in the wake of OxyContin.

Incidentally, opioid abuse is not the only pharmaceutical problem that desperately needs to be addressed by these lawmakers. While many in Appalachia are dying of overdoses, many others can't afford to treat their diabetes or heart conditions or cancer. For an investment of a few million dollars, these pharmaceutical companies are able to make a mint selling deadly drugs to addicts who die because of them, and a second mint selling overpriced drugs to those who will die without them.

While not all that money that flows to politicians comes from manufacturers of OxyContin or other opioid pankillers, the companies that sell addictive opioids do in fact spend a great deal of money to influence lawmakers at the state and federal levels. Over the past 16 years, Purdue Pharma, the maker of OxyContin, has doled out approximately two million dollars in political contributions. One of Purdue's favorite recipients is Senator Richard Burr of North Carolina, who represents a number of Appalachian counties, including my own. They have given Senator Burr thousands of dollars in campaign contributions even though hundreds of his constituents have died from the products Purdue sells. In fact, during the 2016 election cycle, Burr received half of the $20,000 Purdue gave to federal candidates. I wonder if Senator Burr thought about his constituents who die from OxyContin overdoses when his campaign committee got a $10,000 check from Purdue Pharma last year.

Opioids are big business in the states that make up Appalachia. In

TN, KY, NC, and WV, a stunningly high number of opioids are prescribed. The CDC reports the number of opioid prescriptions per 100 residents. In the entire United States, there are almost 83 opioid prescriptions per 100 residents. In NC, the number is 97 per 100. In KY, there are 128 opioid scripts per 100 residents. The numbers are even higher in WV (138/100) and in TN (143/100). If you live in Kentucky, there are enough opioid prescriptions in your community, on average, for every person you know, yourself included, to have at least one. Judging by the numbers, many people have more than one.

When I quipped earlier that OxyContin was a household name in parts of Appalachia, I meant it quite literally. In parts of the region, statistically, every household has a member with a prescription for some form of opioid painkiller.

While OxyContin gets the most attention, it is in many ways a catchall term to describe many other deadly high-powered opiates. There are five major opioid manufacturers: Purdue Pharma, Johnson & Johnson Janssen, Insys, Mylan, and Depomed. These five manufacturers are currently **under investigation** by the United States Senate. Senator Claire McCaskill, a Democrat from Missouri, initiated the investigation. McCaskill has proven to be one of the few voices in Congress willing to go beyond rhetoric and take direct action to hold opioid manufacturers accountable. In announcing the investigation, McCaskill cited the ways prescription opioids have destroyed communities she represents. Her goal is to determine whether or not the five companies under investigation knowingly contributed to the opioid crisis.

It is wholly proper to call the problem a crisis. Between 1999 and 2014, sales of prescription opioids quadrupled in the United States even though data indicates that the amount of reported pain did not increase accordingly. The drug manufacturers were incredibly successful in pitching their opioid painkillers as a magic solution to chronic pain, and we now know that these drug companies **often misled physicians** about the addictive properties of the drugs. People who face crippling pain every day do need access to effective treatments. Those treatments should not come at the expense of their sobriety or their lives, and drug companies should be completely honest both with prescribers and with patients about the addictiveness of their drugs.

As sales of drugs like OxyContin have skyrocketed, so, too, have opioid overdose deaths. Between 2014 and 2015, the core Appalachian states all saw double-digit increases in opioid overdose deaths. In West Virginia, opioid overdose deaths increased by seventeen percent. In Kentucky, the increase was twenty-one percent. These stark statistics are a clear indication that the region is facing an imminent threat. Something must be done, and putting an end to this crisis involves a plan more robust and recovery-oriented than the so-called war on drugs that the government, at all levels, has been blundering for decades. It will take more than militarized police and regional task forces and tough sentences to solve the problem. Only a holistic approach stands any chance at all of succeeding.

As we consider potential solutions to the crisis that continues to unfold in our communities, it is essential that we understand just how complicated the problems are. It is easy to blame the addicts themselves. I know many people who take that approach, and I once thought I understood where they come from. In fact, I once held the opinion myself that addicts simply needed to make better decisions and stop using drugs.

As I watched members of my own immediate family succumb to addiction, I began to realize just how firm a grasp opioids have on those who are addicted to them. Those who are addicted to Vicodin or OxyContin or hydrocodone or fentanyl cannot simply wake up one morning and decide to stop taking the drugs. Even if they are able to overcome the immense mental hold the drugs have on them, there are physical consequences when one stops taking opioids.

Though I rarely speak to her and have not seen her in a number of years, I remember times when my grandmother was unable to get the pills she needed to feed her addiction. Within hours of taking her last pill, she would begin to suffer physically from withdrawal symptoms. The physical withdrawal symptoms made it even more urgent that she find a way to get more pills. When there was nothing of value left to pawn for cash, she would resort to begging anyone who would listen.

Those who take fast-acting opiates – those not designed to be time-released – can experience muscle aches, anxiety, fever, and sweats within just six hours when they run out of pills. Those who go three days without a fix experience nausea, stomach cramps, and diarrhea, among other symptoms. These severe withdrawal symptoms can last for over a week. Usually, just one dose of the opioid from which they are withdrawing can curb the symptoms.

For many addicts, their addictions become a process of maintenance rather than pursuit of a high. As they build up tolerance to the drugs, they are forced to take more and more to get high. Building up a high tolerance for opioids makes addicts more susceptible to overdoses. In many instances, addicts who are arrested and go through detoxification in jail or in a rehabilitation facility return home upon release and immediately begin looking for pills. Sometimes, they will take a dose equal to what they would have taken to get high before their detoxification. However, detoxing often lowers their tolerance, and they are no longer able to tolerate the same amount of drugs they were able to just weeks before. The result, in many instances, is an accidental overdose.

So often, those of us who have never been addicts ourselves react by shaming those who struggle with addiction. We hesitate to speak aloud the realities that most others already know when those close to us are addicts. That shame extends for addicts even to death. Rather than being candid when our loved ones die of overdoses, we try to pretend they met a different fate. Rarely does one see an obituary that lists drug overdose as the cause of death. We don't talk about it because we are ashamed to.

Perhaps if we were more candid both with ourselves and with our neighbors, we might begin to understand that we have more in common than we realize. One of the most important parts of recovery, I think, is community. Addicts need to know that they are accepted and loved, not that they are shamed or outcast. Those of us whose family members struggle with addiction need to know that many of our neighbors are struggling in the same ways, too.

We must stop blaming addicts for being addicted. So many cultural, economic, and mental health realities that are far beyond the control of addicts conspire to prevent them from a neat recovery no matter how dedicated they are to healing. Perhaps the most important part of recovery apart from a supportive community and access to proper mental and physical healthcare is hope. In so many parts of Appalachia, there's little to give addicts hope. In fact, it's that desperation – that hopelessness – that often leads them to drugs in the first place. As we continue to think through how we should react to this crisis, we have to look deeper than the drugs or the addiction.

Getting pharmaceutical companies out of the community-killing business is a lofty goal. Perhaps we start by demanding that our elected representatives stand up to drug companies instead of just talking tough then taking campaign contributions from big pharma when they think we aren't looking. Some will argue that when prescription opiates go away, addicts will turn back to heroin or meth to feed their addictions. They are likely right. However, it seems disingenuous at best that we use such a terrible excuse to avoid holding multi-national corporations accountable for peddling poison to vulnerable communities.

We must understand that the addiction plaguing our mountains is simply a reaction to a much deeper set of problems. Addicts are usually driven to drugs because they think getting high or dying are the only ways to escape the hopelessness and misery they face every day of their lives. Until we get serious about addressing the systemic poverty in our region, at its roots, our family members and our neighbors stand little chance of beating the cycle of intergenerational addiction. They need hope, and hope comes from being valued as humans. America at large has little use for white trash, and we tend to put drug addicts squarely into this category. Only when we think of our addicted neighbors as neighbors and not throwaway humans will we start to truly understand what we need to do to put our communities back together.

You Are Not An Impostor

June 26, 2017

I have suffered from Imposter Syndrome all my life. It still shows up sometimes, usually unexpectedly, though I am getting better at believing the title of this essay. I continue to modify this essay every semester and share it with students who need to know that they are not imposters. If you know students like this, I hope you'll share it with them, too.

You belong here.

Today, for the second summer in a row, I begin teaching in Western Carolina University's Summer Learning Communities programs. My first class this afternoon will consist of students from the university's Academic Success Program. ASP is a conditional admission program meaning that the students who participate do not qualify for standard admission to the university. They come for a five-week program at the end of summer where they take two general studies courses and a transitions course. If they complete the summer experience successfully, they are granted admission to the university in the fall. Those three words, "you belong here," will be the cornerstone of my introduction to the students this afternoon. It occurs to me, though, that I find myself saying those words every semester even to those whose admission is not conditional and who are by most measures exceptional students. They are words that, I hope, someone would have said to me had I been able to afford to go to college at 18.

If you are a first generation college student, you might find yourself struggling after a few weeks of college with the notion that you don't belong there. If you suffer from mental or physical illness, or come from an abusive home or relationship, or struggle with a learning disability, you might find yourself wondering if you have what it takes to finish a degree or a semester or a class or even one more day on campus. When those voices of doubt begin their hateful chorus in your head, just keep telling yourself: you belong here.

For much of my life, when something good happened to me, no matter how hard I worked for it, I immediately found myself scared and worried. It was often hard for me to celebrate my successes because I didn't believe I deserved them. I often thought that my achievements were a series of accidents. Eventually, I feared, the world would catch on and know that I shouldn't have accomplished the things I had. I thought I didn't deserve the good things and it didn't matter that I had worked my ass off for them.

I came to realize that those fears had a name: imposter syndrome. I struggled with it all of my life until I encountered mentors who understood it and worked to help me overcome it. When I finally realized what it was, I began to understand that it was a sort of artifact left over in my mind from having grown up poor.

Today, only rarely do I find myself slipping into the rut of imposter syndrome. I have become substantially more confident in large part because of the way those around me - my wife, my in-laws, a few members of my family, my colleagues, and those who taught me in undergrad and in graduate school - reinforce the idea that I deserve the things I work to earn. Because I experienced it so often in my life, I am generally better able to see it in my students, and my heart silently breaks every time I talk to a student who thinks they don't belong simply because of where they came from.

My own journey in higher education didn't begin until I was 31. I dreamed for years about going to college, but I couldn't afford to go after high school, and once I started building a career in business, I saw no way to leave my business to go to school. Finally, in 2010, when I found myself burned out and struggling after the Great Recession, I decided it was time to change my life. I sold my business and spent a year working up the courage to enroll in college. I planned it all very carefully, but even the most detailed plans didn't erase my anxiety.

I was a terrible student in junior high and high school. I never made above a D in math, and I didn't apply myself in the ways I should have, often because I was so paralyzed by the stigma associated with being poor. I looked around and saw that most of the "smart" kids around me wore nice name-brand clothing. They went on fun vacations and their parents had nice cars and they wore Nike shoes. Because I lacked all those things, my teenage brain thought I lacked the same intellectual capacity as them, too.

These fears continued to haunt me as I timidly considered going to college. For years, I operated in business with ego and bravado, but it was mostly a facade. That facade finally cracked, though I tried to hide that fact from those around me. The truth is that the prospect of going to college terrified me not because I didn't want to go - I wanted it more than anything - but because I thought I wasn't good enough to succeed.

Eventually, I decided that I would try it even if I wasn't certain how it would turn out. I started out at the local community college, and continued to believe I would fail miserably. Then, a couple of weeks into the semester, I realized how much I loved learning. By that time, I had begun to get feedback in the form of grades. Those grades were all A's, and they were salve for my anxious mind. I remember the first day of statistics, the class I feared most. I admitted on my first-day questionnaire that I was terrible at math and feared I would fail the class. The instructor, Hilary Seagle, wrote "we'll work on it together, then," and returned it to me. I'm not sure Hilary knows how much good she did me with those six words, or how grateful I am for them even now. I finished the class with a 97 average. It turns out that I wasn't a shitty student anymore. Twelve months after I first stepped foot into a college classroom, I finished an Associate of Arts degree with a 4.0 GPA.

After graduating from Southwestern Community College, I enrolled at Western Carolina University, and the same old fears returned. I convinced myself that my work at the community college was a fluke, and that I couldn't succeed at the university. Once again, I was wrong. At WCU, I met amazing professors who simultaneously scared the hell out of me and inspired me to be a better student. By the time I finished Dr. Alex Macaulay's Sophomore Seminar in History, I knew that I wanted to be a college professor. I finally found the courage to admit that I was NOT an imposter. Thanks to Dr. Macaulay and so many others, I found my place. For the first time in my life, I felt like I belonged. I determined then that I would make it my primary goal to someday help my students get there, too.

Failure is generally an objective measure. You will not have failed simply because you feel like a failure. When those imposter syndrome demons come for you, think of where you are now. If you are farther along now than you once were, even if the path to here really sucked, know that that progress is meaningful. I grew up in a world where I considered myself to be white trash because I thought that's how others saw me. Today, I'm teaching at a wonderful college that I never thought I'd even get the privilege to attend. I take credit for very little of this, because so many have bolstered my hard work with grace and kindness and encouragement. But I know this: the fact that I am here is not an accident. I no longer go to sleep at night fearing that I'll somehow be discovered as a fraud and stripped of all I have accomplished.

So, if you find yourself reading this because someone saw it on the internet and thought it might fit your circumstances, let me tell you: you belong here. Wherever here is. If you worked your ass off to get where you are, know that you deserve to be there. If other people reached out to pull you up along the way, you still deserve to be there, and you owe it to those who helped you not only to say "thank you," but to now reach back yourself and help others who are struggling as you once struggled.

Poverty, Privilege, and the Dead American Dream

June 28, 2017

As expected, I got some push-back when I published this essay. There are those who still refuse to believe that certain Americans (namely those of color and those who are impoverished) lack access to the same opportunities as their white and more affluent neighbors. This is, I realize, an uncomfortable reality, but the fact that it makes some uncomfortable makes it no less true.

Once upon a time, I believed in the American Dream.

In fact, I once believed myself to be living proof that it existed. I bought into the notion that if one worked hard enough, one could be upwardly mobile no matter the adversity they faced. I thought that the only limitations to achievement in the United States were laziness and stupidity. I looked around me at all the people who were not achieving some form of the American Dream and decided that they were to blame for their circumstances. I had worked hard to get what I wanted, and even though I often struggled with Impostor Syndrome, I didn't waiver in my belief that only lack of initiative prevented most folks from achieving greatness.

The truth is, I had so many examples in my own life that debunked the star-spangled spectacular mythos of the American Dream that, looking back, I find it laughable that I ever thought prosperity was available to everyone who wanted to work for it. It took me a long time to realize that my rosy view of the American Dream was a result of my own privilege.

I would bet someone a cheeseburger lunch at Cosmic Carryout that when I post this essay on my personal Facebook page, I will get push-back about mentioning white privilege within an hour. I get it. I was hesitant for a long time to admit the existence of white privilege, too. If you are a regular reader of my essays, you know a good bit about how I grew up. In short, we didn't have much, and I know I missed out on opportunities as a result. It was hard for me to reconcile how I could possibly have any sort of privilege when I came from a socioeconomic class that seems anything but privileged.

Some years ago, I was in the radio business, and I remember being struck by a public service announcement distributed by the Ad Council. In the ad, a voice actor calls the same number repeatedly to inquire about a Park Avenue apartment for rent. He calls using various voices meant to represent different racial and ethnic groups, and every time, the person answering the phone quickly informs him that the apartment has been rented. Finally, he calls using his real voice and purporting to be "Graeme Wellington." The rental agent is happy to give him information even though she previously told him, when he portrayed himself as African American, Indian, and Hispanic, that the apartment had been rented.

I'm certain that the piece was dramatized, but it made me start to think about how real discrimination is. Finally, I realized that simply by virtue of being a white male I automatically have the privilege to ignore certain issues because they do not affect me personally. It was easy to pretend that racism, discrimination, sexism, and bigotry didn't exist because those things didn't hurt me. That's white privilege, and even if I couldn't afford the apartment in question, the rental agent might be more likely to take my call simply because I sound white and have a white name. (Incidentally, isn't it sort of fascinating that we know enough about what it means to "sound white" or "sound black" that we can all understand what is happening in the PSA? We are programmed to understand stereotypes even if we do not agree with them.)

When we take the time to understand that white privilege does in fact exist and admit that it is a factor at play in US society whether we like it or not, it becomes easier to understand other forms of privilege. The concept of privilege helps us understand not only poverty but the ways Americans access or are prohibited from accessing the American Dream.

One of the most important lessons we can learn from history is this: there are exceptions to everything. Certainly there were incidents of African Americans fighting for the South during the US Civil War. That does not mean that most, or even many, African Americans believed in the Confederate cause. Some labor activists came to the South from the North to unionize cotton mills, but that doesn't mean that all labor activists were "outside agitators." There are some frozen yogurt machines labeled "chocolate" that actually dispense vanilla froyo. That doesn't mean you should distrust every froyo dispenser automatically. There's almost an unlimited number of circumstances and configurations that prove that universalizing based on a limited number of occurrences is not wise.

Both privilege and universalization help us to explain the fallacies of so many of the arguments surrounding poverty in the United States. Those who have never pulled themselves out of poverty have very little insight into what it takes to make this happen. Having not experienced it themselves, it is difficult to understand how or why some people are able to lift themselves out of inter-generational poverty. That is not to say that they cannot sympathize or even empathize with those who do. However, what often happens is that someone who doesn't understand firsthand what it takes to recover from poverty begins to think that if some people can do it than anyone should be able to.

The stark reality is that climbing out of poverty is highly unlikely today in the United States. Increasingly, demographics indicate that Americans tend to remain in the social classes into which they are born. Those who are born poor tend to stay that way even when they attain higher education. A recent study by economists Michael Carr and Emily Wiemers noted that upward mobility between classes is increasingly unlikely. That is not to say it is entirely unlikely. I managed to escape poverty. I know many others who did, too. That does not mean that everyone can.

It is easy for those of us who found a way out of poverty to be self-congratulatory. After all, we truly have accomplished something important. We have changed our lives, generally for the better. Few of us got here on our own, but most of us invested time, energy, and emotion in making it happen. Most of us worked for it, and that is an incredibly respectable reality. Those of us who elevated ourselves out of the lower classes now have privilege, and it is essential that we not let that privilege blind us to those around us who lack that privilege.

Recently, a reader responded to one of my essays via social media. She asked how I managed to elevate myself out of poverty. The truth is, I don't know. I wish I did. I wish I had some magic formula, because I would replicate it and give it away to the masses. No two instances of poverty are the same, and therefore no single method of escape from it is universal.

Southern author Rick Bragg said that he climbed up his mother's backbone and out of poverty. That's probably as close an explanation as I will ever find to explain my own situation. I don't know that I have ever met anyone who found a way out of poverty without the help of others. Sometimes, it is those who have the least to give who are the most helpful. Sometimes, the best and most useful help doesn't come in the form of money or resources, but sometimes it does. Sometimes, knowing that somebody gives a damn about you and wants you to succeed is the first step. Sometimes, we are so busy fighting the soul-crushing poverty we see all around us that we end up in a better place and have absolutely no clue how it happened. And sometimes, we feel guilty because we escaped while those we love the most did not.

What I have come to know is this. I am the owner of a whole lot of privilege, and even though I started out at a disadvantage compared to many, I have had some form of privilege for my entire life. In addition to my status as a white male with an advanced degree, I have a platform from which I am able to reach thousands of people every month. With privilege comes responsibility. For me personally, that means that the highest and best use of my own privilege is not necessarily to use it only to advance myself. For me, it means I am called to use it as a means of reaching back to those who lack privilege to be an advocate and an ally. And for me, that usually means researching and writing about poverty and those who are impoverished, using my own life experiences as a guide.

So many of those who speak from positions of privilege cite the American Dream as the mechanism by which all people in the US have the opportunity to escape poverty. The existence of this piece of American mythology has been used for ages to justify victim-blaming. If the American Dream is something that exists and is functional, then there's no reason why people have to remain poor, right? If there is a standard process through which Americans from all socioeconomic classes find upward mobility, then there must exist some formulaic set of behaviors or actions which, if followed, result in prosperity and success. However, this is not the case. If it were, then everyone who works hard and does the "right" things would be upwardly mobile. At some point, we must admit the grim reality that some people, no matter how hard they work and no matter how many times they make the socially-agreed-upon right choice, will remain impoverished their entire lives. To them, the American Dream is nothing but a fantasy.

I'm not sure there has ever been a time when access to the American Dream has been universal. I'm also not sure it remains productive to continue to cite it as an appropriate response when discussing poverty. It puts the blame on the victim in many cases. One is forced either to admit that some people lack access to the American Dream or to blame those who can't access it for some unnamed shortcoming that prevented them from upward mobility.

As for me, I am not comfortable with a set of systems in which it is usually only a fortunate accident when someone from the lowest rungs of the socioeconomic ladder are able to find their way up to a higher rung. When we critically assess the state of the American Dream in 2017, we quickly realize that it is neither a panacea not an excuse to prevent us from making the hard systemic changes necessary to end poverty.

My Mother's Keeper

August 7, 2017

Originally published under the title "Do Broken People Matter?," this is the most personal thing I have ever shared publicly. This story serves, in part, as the basis for a book I'm currently writing tentatively titled My Mother Wasn't Trash.

I remember the day I became my mother's keeper.

I was 22, and she had recently left her fourth husband. She and I decided it made sense for the two of us to share a place for a while, so we rented a little house and moved in together. It was the first time since I had left home on my eighteenth birthday that I had the chance to be around her for extended periods of time.

Until that point, I had only a vague idea of the extent of her mental and physical illnesses, and I didn't realize that her condition was truly debilitating. I knew for most of my life that she would sometimes take pills and often smoked pot, but I never thought of her as an addict. Her recreational drug use had never interfered with her ability to work an endless assortment of shitty dead-end jobs and, after graduating from a technical school, slightly less shitty entry-level office jobs. By the time she moved in with me that summer, she even had a job with health insurance, a first for her.

As her suffering increased, so did her drive to seek drugs to numb the pain. She began complaining more often that none of the drugs her doctor prescribed were helpful in dulling her chronic pain.

One evening, one of her friends came to visit, and minutes after she arrived, the two of them locked themselves in the bathroom of the sad little house we were renting. For some reason, there was only one thing on my mind in that moment: Meth. Knowing her friend's background and lifestyle, I became certain that she was introducing my mother to a drug that I believed was a death sentence. The drug had just begun its heartbreaking takeover of Appalachia. I had no clue what it looked like or even how it was used, but I knew what it did to people.

I knocked on the bathroom door, and when they yelled at me to go away, I lowered my elbow and pushed through the door with all my weight. When I replay it in my head, I can still hear the sickening crack and snap of the cheap door fame as it yielded to my weight.

My suspicions were confirmed by the small mirror lying on the counter, dirtied with white powder, and the rolled up dollar bill in my mother's hand. In that moment, the weight of the world settled onto my shoulders.

She was angrier at me than I had ever seen her. She told me that what they were doing was none of my business, and that she was a grown-assed woman, and she'd do whatever she wanted. Her friend cursed me and I cursed right back. The two of them stomped out the door in a hurry.

As I sat on the porch in the minutes after her friend's car left our driveway, my head spun, my mind raced, and I realized that it was up to me to try to save her. There wasn't anyone else. I suppose I was still young enough and naïve enough to think I could rescue her. I didn't really know anything about mental illness or addiction, but life was about to hand me an education in both.

I drove to her friend's house, pulled into the driveway, and blasted the horn until a man I had never met came out and asked what I wanted. I demanded that he tell Libby that it was time to go. He shuffled back in, and in a few minutes, mom walked out and got into the car with me. In my adrenaline-filled rush, I didn't consider how stupid it was to drive up to a house I knew to be filled with drugs and honk the horn and make demands. I didn't think to be scared for my own safety. I was just worried about my mom.

On the way home, she sobbed and asked me to forgive her. I didn't admit that I was scared. I was pretending to be a badass without emotions, but I did forgive her. In truth, I could barely keep from shaking from the adrenaline and fear pulsing through my veins. It's as if the drugs she had taken were having some physiological effect on me, too.

By the time we got home, she was done crying. She started screaming and throwing things and demanded that I drive her back to her friend's house. I still remember the sound of an ashtray crashing into her dresser mirror, and the feeling of her warm wet tears soaking the right shoulder of my shirt when I grabbed her in a bear hug, told her I loved her, and asked her to calm down. Years later, I would realize that she was exhibiting textbook signs of bipolar disorder that night. At the time, I assumed it was whatever cocktail of drugs she had ingested.

The next day, she left again. She said she'd never speak to me again if I tried to come get her, but she promised to let me know she was safe. She also promised that she wouldn't touch meth again, but I didn't believe her. She called every few days, always at unpredictable hours, usually slurring her words, but occasionally hyper and full of big plans.

I decided I would throw myself into my work, because I didn't know what else to do and I still had bills to pay. She apparently had the opposite notion and left the best job she ever had, either voluntarily or involuntarily. I never got a clear answer, and I'm not sure I want one.

About a month after she left, she stopped calling, then her phone started going straight to voicemail when I dialed her number. Eventually, I got a collect call from the county jail. Because she had taken up residence at her friend's house, she was arrested when the police busted down the door one evening and found an assortment of illegal substances. Her friend paid her bail, I paid the lawyer, and a few months later, they dropped the charges against my mother.

She came back home for a while, then reconnected with a man she once knew who would soon become husband number five (and six – long story).

Not long after the events described above, through a series of lucky business opportunities, I bought a business in eastern Kentucky and moved there to run it. Mom decided that she wanted to come, too, so I paid for an apartment for she and number five and paid her a small salary from my business despite her inability to do meaningful work because of her chronic pain.

Just a few months after moving to Kentucky, husband number five decided he had had enough and moved back to North Carolina. I paid for the divorce and we bid him adieu. Mom became unstable again, and one evening after getting a cryptic text message from her, I went to her apartment to find her passed out on her bed, blood dripping from her left wrist. She had tried to take her own life.

At the hospital, she agreed that it would be best if she sought inpatient psychiatric care. In rural Kentucky, however, mental health infrastructure is severely lacking at best and cruel at worst. I'm not sure her week-long stay at a hospital where the staff treated her like trash did anything at all to help her. Little did I know at the time that this incident would not be the last time she would attempt suicide or the last time she would spend time in an inpatient psychiatric facility.

In the years that followed, she attempted suicide at least five more times. Twice, I had to initiate involuntary commitment because she refused to seek the help she so desperately needed. Eventually, she was able to get diagnoses for many of her mental health problems. She suffered from severe bipolar disorder and anxiety. With these diagnoses came medication regimens that were helpful so long as she took her medicine as prescribed. This was not always the case.

Though she never turned back to meth, so far as I know, she managed to find physicians who would give her virtually any kind of pills she wanted, often with little concern for how the drugs would impact her mental health. There was no denying the extent of her physical illnesses. I once paid for an MRI that showed, in stunning detail, the assortment of disintegrated and otherwise destroyed discs in her lower back and in her neck. In an effort to treat her physical problems, she was often prescribed drugs that made her mental health worse.

In particular, the sedative Klonopin caused her to have severe emotional reactions. She was taking this drug at least five of the six times she attempted to take her own life. Each time, she would admit afterward that Klonopin took her to what she described as a "dark place." She would always flush the remainder of her prescription when she got home from the hospital, but something drove her, time and again, to ask her doctors for new prescriptions for Klonopin. Eventually, I called her doctor and explained the correlation between the drug and her suicide attempts and told him he would be acting irresponsibly if he ever gave it to her again.

The last time she attempted to kill herself, her doctor, despite my previous warning, had just given her a new prescription for Klonopin. After I got mom to the hospital, I called the doctor, and I have never said such horrible words to another human as I said to him. I told him that if my mother died, he would have blood on his hands. She agreed later to never see this doctor again, but he still practices medicine in our hometown.

A few months ago, I wrote a bit about my mother's life, and I continue to be stunned by the response. Over 650,000 people have read my essay titled "My Mother Wasn't Trash," and every day new people reach out to tell me that her story has touched them in some way.

Because of the apparent power of vulnerability, and because so many people have found my mother's story to be helpful in understanding the world around them, I think it is appropriate that I continue to use her story as a lens through which to view Appalachia and the region's problems.

There are many problems in Appalachia so widespread as to be systematic, and most of them can be examined, in some way, through examining my mother's life. Two in particular are of urgent importance given what is unfolding in our region now. Addiction and mental health are so deeply intertwined in Appalachian (and, I suppose, in much of America) as to be inseparable, and both have reached crisis level in our region.

The thing is, we don't like talking about either. We attach shame and stigma and blame to both mental illness and addiction, and even though almost every family in Appalachia is in some way touched by both, many of us like to go about our lives pretending that our families are safe from the unpleasantness that is rotting our communities.

It's time we stop lying to ourselves and plastering over reality with rainbows-and-unicorns bullshit and start talking about it, even if it hurts. Actually, especially if it hurts.

When I first wrote about my mother and published it publicly on my blog, I took no pleasure in sharing such intimate details about my life. While I was not embarrassed, I was hesitant to share a story so personal. The first time I got an email from someone telling me that my mother's story sounds just like their own, I realized the power of shared experience. I decided that I would continue telling the stories of Appalachian people as a means of speaking truth to power. When those who could bring about change are confronted with the truth – that is, with hard, unvarnished, raw, emotional reality – it is harder for them to ignore us.

My mother was ignored for just about all of her life. Now that she is gone and I'm telling her story, I realize that there's too much at stake to allow our region to be ignored, or, worse, stereotyped, universalized, and rolled in a simplistic narrative heavy on victim-blaming. I am tired of seeing my neighbors and friends and family members deprived of their humanity, stripped down to nothing but white trash stereotypes, and treated differently because of the conditions into which they were born.

The truth is, even for the first few years after I realized I had become my mother's keeper, I thought she could fix herself if only she would try hard enough. I bought into the false narrative of "personal responsibility" that is so prevalent in American political dialogue. I believed that those who were poor were poor because they didn't work hard enough. I thought those who were addicted were addicted because they didn't want to stop using drugs. I thought that those who suffered from mental health problems, especially depression, should just learn to think differently. I am ashamed that I ever thought this way. I was wrong, and I could have taken better care of my mother had I bothered to stop and listen to her and those like her.

So here we are, in 2017, talking in terms sometimes abstract and sometimes personal, about poverty, addiction, and mental illness. President Trump has at times shown interest in addressing the opioid crisis that is shaking the foundations of rural America. Politicians, some more successfully and seriously than others, are showing interest in addressing the challenges of healthcare access. Few are talking about America's mental health crisis, though, and this is the key to understanding the first two. We will never begin to solve the opioid epidemic or address healthcare until we come to terms with the way we view mental illness.

Here is the problem, as plainly as I know how to state it: addiction is a mental illness, yet we treat it like a crime or a character flaw. Mental healthcare IS healthcare.

What's more, those with other mental illnesses, in particular depression, bipolar disorder, and post-traumatic stress disorder, are sometimes more likely to abuse drugs because of their mental health conditions. The result is that if we have any hope at all of addressing the plague of drug abuse in rural areas in any meaningful way, we MUST invest in mental health infrastructure. If large swaths of middle-class America were suffering systematically from some sort of physical impairment, all manner of funding would be focused on bringing expertise and resources to those areas to fix the impairment.

In the poorer parts of the US, however, no one is coming. It doesn't matter if it's poisoned water in Flint, Michigan or Oxycontin overdoses in Oceana, West Virginia. It seems, at least on the national level, that no one is interested in treating crises in impoverished communities with the same urgency as crises in middle-class America. I have known all my life that poor lives matter less than rich ones. Our approach to solving the opioid crisis is just more piece of evidence.

Many of the proposed solutions coming out of Washington rely on the tried-and-failed "law and order" approach. That is, addicts, and those who support their addictions by selling drugs, are criminals, and therefore increased law enforcement effort is the best way to solve the problem. According to these folks, the proper approach is to clean up the streets, lock the addicts and dealers up so they can't dirty up our neighborhoods, and push the problem back out of sight. This approach is so wrong as to border on immoral.

When I consider potential solutions, I cannot help but revisit my mother's story. Chronic pain and a lifetime of mental and physical abuse were likely the two most important factors that led her to abuse drugs. I wholeheartedly believe she was seeking relief from chronic pain, but I also realize that she was seeking relief from chronic heartbreak and mental anguish, too.

People like my mother reach a point where they realize the hopelessness of their situations. As I have written previously, there are many who can make all the least-shitty choices in a life of shitty options and still end up mired in poverty with no means of escaping. When they do all the things society tells them they should – work hard, get an education, work harder, get a second or third job – yet still end up with no path to the middle class, they just give up. For these folks – and my mother was one of them – sometimes the temporary escape provided by drugs is the only respite they can find from an unjust world seemingly stacked against them.

I do not know what it is like to have such severe physical pain that I would be tempted to try meth just to make it go away. Neither do I know what it is like to suffer from mental illness that is only made worse by attempts to make the physical pain more bearable. What I do know is that most people who have never experienced these realities firsthand tend to think it must somehow be the fault of those suffering.

To be clear, my mother made the decision to take drugs, both prescribed and illegal. However, she did not make the choice to be poor, or to have her back broken by degrading manual labor for minimum wage. She made plenty of tough choices over the course of her life in response to crises she never asked for. Her choices certainly shaped her life, but not nearly as much as it was shaped by the things in her life that were utterly beyond her control.

I'm not convinced that personal choices end up making a bit of difference for people like my mother. Really, the only truly life-changing decisions they make revolve around how long they are going to try before they give up. Some end up trying until the day they die of natural causes. Some give up by pushing the plunger of an over-loaded needle. Some, like my mother, try over and over, unsuccessfully, to make the pain stop for good. At some point, the date of their death is the only remaining turning point they can control.

As we consider the path forward, we must begin understanding addiction, mental health, hopelessness, and poverty as part of the same broken system. We cannot continue to address these problems piecemeal and expect positive outcomes.

One of the first things we must address is access to quality mental health care. This is particularly problematic in rural areas. Often, addicts end up in the emergency rooms of their local hospitals because drug abuse has threatened their physical health. Once they are medically cleared, they are often sent home. Perhaps, if they are lucky, they leave the ER with a referral to a local mental health provider.

Rural community mental health practitioners are some of the most caring and giving people I know, but they usually lack appropriate levels funding to provide the evidence-based care that they know will lead to better outcomes for addicts and those with severe mental health issues.

If our current national conversations about the opioid epidemic lead to plans for action, we must first address our lack of willingness to fund mental health treatment. That would, of course, require acknowledging that opioid addiction is, according to the American Psychological Association's Diagnosis and Statistics Manual, a legitimate mental health diagnosis. I believe wholeheartedly that many Americans are not quite ready to stop blaming addicts for their addiction and start agreeing to use their tax money to pay for solutions.

Addiction touches families both rich and poor, but, like most other mental and physical illnesses, outcomes differ based on socioeconomic situation. Those from wealthy families have the resources to seek out voluntary inpatient addiction treatment. Those from impoverished families rely on whatever piecemeal treatment they can get from outpatient community mental health, and usually, the only treatment available to them is that paid for by Medicaid.

Even for those who suffer from mental illness but who are not addicts, access to proper mental health treatment is severely lacking in most parts of Appalachia. Sometimes, local family practitioners offer the only access many patients have to mental health treatment. Faced with no other viable options, it seems, some physicians will prescribe antidepressants as a desperate means of helping their suffering patients. Those patients who do seek inpatient care sometimes end up in situations like my mother, locked up in hellish psychiatric wards in terribly underfunded hospitals that are more like punishment than therapy.

None of the solutions are simple. They require changing hearts and minds, and they rely on political action that comes often in the form of increased funding. When we consider that truly addressing income inequality in the US would do much to address addiction and mental illness, the solutions become even more complicated. However, if we acknowledge that outcomes for those suffering from mental health problems and addiction usually vary based on socioeconomic status (and there's plenty of peer-reviewed proof of this), it becomes clear that the poor are not given the same opportunities for treatment as the middle class or the wealthy.

In the end, I think we have to ask ourselves a hard question: Do these people matter? Do those who suffer from opioid addiction or bipolar disorder or PTSD or some combination of addiction and other mental illness really matter? If people like my mother do not matter in the grand scheme of American society, then let's just move on. If they do matter, however, then we have to keep asking hard questions and looking for impossible answers.

JOSHUA WILKEY

Ticonderoga Pencils and Poverty

September 24, 2017

In this essay, I examine something I call "artifacts of poverty." In ways evident and invisible, poverty is rarely gone even when those experiencing it have ascended to a higher socioeconomic class.

When I was a kid, I didn't get Ticonderoga pencils very often.

The reality is that my mom usually couldn't afford Ticonderoga pencils. Instead, I got whatever was cheapest. It makes sense, really. When pot roast is a treat rather than a regular dinner, it seems foolish to pay extra for something like pencils. Say what you want about poor people and the seemingly stupid financial decisions they make – and my mother certainly made her fair share over the years – but they understand scarcity.

I don't think I realized just what a lasting impact this mindset had on my life until just a few years ago. My wife was not yet my wife, and she and I had just gotten serious about one another. We were buying groceries together for the first time. When I suggested that we grill some hot dogs for dinner, she agreed, asked me what kind we should get, and said that her default was Oscar Mayer. Without even thinking about it, I had already begun to reach for the disgusting red store brand, and I told her that I my default was still poverty. We chuckled, but it was at that moment I realized that while I had left poverty, poverty never really left me.

I have come to call those things that still lurk somewhere in the back of my mind the "artifacts of poverty." Even though they are not necessarily present on the surface, in the right circumstances, they still present themselves. Sometimes they come out unexpectedly. Sometimes, I don't even realize how much of my daily behavior is influenced by having grown up in an environment of scarcity. I still hesitate to fill my car fully with gas. I prefer shopping several times a month for groceries rather than stocking up once a month.

Neither of these things are rational, because we have a very comfortable middle-class life. Filling up with gas isn't going to deprive us of food later in the week, and spending a couple hundred bucks on groceries at the beginning of the month isn't going to leave us without money for an extra or unexpected bill later in the month. However, I have been so socially conditioned by poverty that my focus is still on surviving today, and maybe tomorrow.

I am incredibly fortunate that this is no longer the reality for me, and it will hopefully never be the reality for Betsy and I as we build our family. However, the fact that I am no longer poor does not mean I no longer think about it. I'm not really scarred by it, but I am compelled to think about it because even today, there are kids in our community who are experiencing the same systems of scarcity that so deeply influenced me when I was a kid.

I become acutely aware of how much my life has changed since then when I think about our household shopping patterns. I am also reminded, when I think of these changes, just how severely the deck is stacked against the poor and working poor in our current economy.

Betsy and I are frequent users of Amazon Prime. It pains me to admit this, given our love for and support of small and local businesses. I know Amazon's business model is harmful to smaller businesses, which is why we do not shop at Amazon with a clear conscience. However, in our rural community, we have little choice apart from Walmart for household essentials. We cannot procure many of the organic or healthy retail items in our kitchen without driving an hour or taking time off work to shop at the single limited-hours health foods store in our community. For us, it is easier and cheaper to throw things into our Amazon cart and have them shipped, at no cost, right to our door.

In addition to the convenience, we also save a whole lot of money by buying many of our essentials via Amazon. I wear Dickies brand pants to work in the woodshop and in the yard, and I can get them for around twenty bucks a pair on Amazon. If they have my size in stock at the local Walmart, they are nearly $28. I paid $18 this spring for a good pair of chicken coop boots, but the cheapest I could find them locally was almost three times that amount. All told, we save at least several hundred dollars a year shopping via Amazon, not counting the free two-day shipping. For this privilege, we pay $99/year.

My mother could have benefitted from a convenient discount retailer like Amazon Prime, but even if it had have existed in my childhood, she couldn't have afforded a membership. She used to talk about how wonderful it would be to shop at Sam's Club, but she acknowledged that she had neither the money for a membership nor the cash flow to be able to buy anything in bulk. Discount retailing like Amazon Prime and Sam's Club, you see, is reserved for those who can afford it. Isn't that a hell of a paradox?

Those who didn't grow up in poverty really can't understand the daily realities of being a poor kid. Many who grew up poor, it seems, have purposefully or inadvertently forgotten how hard it is to be an impoverished child. In the decades following the Great Depression, we came to value the stories of those who escaped poverty, and many of those who managed to escape it began to argue that even though they grew up poor, everyone else around them was also poor, so they didn't really know. This is not my reality, and I'm relatively confident that it isn't the reality of many of those who tell their stories that way, either. Somewhere along the way, when we can afford Amazon Prime and Oscar Mayer hotdogs, we assume that our becoming able to do so was inevitable. As a result, we sometimes forget the very real struggles of those around us whose stories have not unfolded in the same way.

I have been able to afford good hot dogs for a whole lot of years, but sometimes, I still find those artifacts of poverty hiding somewhere deep inside my mind. I can also afford nice office supplies, and I started buying Ticonderoga pencils as soon as I started working. Truth be known, I should have probably stuck with the crappy store-brand pencils during the first few years of my working life, because I was certainly still eating cheap hotdogs. For me, though, using a Ticonderoga pencil was a statement. I suppose it still is.

In so many ways, a Ticonderoga pencil is a powerful symbol for children. Today, they are about a quarter each when purchased from Amazon, and even more expensive when purchased locally. The cheapest pencils are a third of that price, and even cheaper during back-to-school sales at Walmart. Therefore, Ticonderogas still represent a class divide for children who shouldn't have to think about class.

Much like poverty in general, I was often very aware that my school supplies were cheaper than what most of my classmates had. It wasn't just the pencils. I got cheap notebooks and cheap backpacks. My shoes were cheap, and my clothes sometimes came from secondhand stores.

Even if it was more my perception than the reality, I remember feeling like I was inferior because the stuff I had wasn't as good as the stuff most of my classmates had. That sort of thing weighs on a kid. In today's social-media-and-consumerism society, I can't imagine how much worse it must be for the kids whose parents can't afford the nice things.

These days, when I pick up my Ticonderoga pencil, I am reminded of the journey I have made over the last 36 years. Neither of my parents finished high school, but I am a college professor with three college degrees and a fourth in progress. Even though Ticonderogas were a rare treat, I learned how to use a pencil pretty effectively anyway as evidenced by my own academic and professional successes. Somewhere inside me, though, is the second grader who worried himself into a headache almost every day because he was able to look around and know that almost everyone around him had better stuff. Somewhere very near you, too, is a second grader whose parents can't afford nice pencils and who feels inferior because of it. What will you do about it?

Surprised by Trump's Popularity in Appalachia? Don't Be.

October 18, 2017

I often find myself pissed off by the hordes of "Trump Whisperers" who parade through the cable news channels attempting to explain why us poor dumb hillbillies voted for the Cheeto in Chief. This essay was my attempt to explain the historical and political context for Trump's popularity in Appalachia.

For those of us who study Appalachia's politics, Trumps popularity comes as no surprise.

Appalachia has long existed outside the economic norms of the United States, and often, it exists outside the norms of American politics, too. The result is that it is sometimes difficult for those who are not from the region, or who haven't studied it carefully, to understand the region's politics.

Because a full 95% of the counties in Appalachia swung toward Trump in the election, many were shocked when the President's first budget proposal sought to slash government agencies and programs thought to be vital to the region. The Roanoke Times declared: "Trump backhands Appalachia." USA Today argued that "Trump budget beats down Appalachia." In my own back yard, the Asheville Citizen-Times was less aggressive: "Trump's proposed budget has Appalachia worried."

I understand why people question the seemingly unwavering support of Trump's candidacy (and now, his presidency), by folks in Appalachia. Plenty of ink has been spilled since November by various writers and journalists attempting to explain the phenomenon. For some, it boils down to a single issue: coal. For others, it is about elitism. Perhaps the most common argument is that supporting Trump is a sort of hail-Mary pass aimed at economic survival or improvement.

There's truth in all of these arguments, but there are also other forces at play. Many of those who continue to question the logic of Appalachia so heartily supporting Trump live outside the region and lack the historical or cultural context to understand the complex processes that drive Appalachian politics.

In many ways, those who point to elitism as the root of Appalachia's disdain for Democratic political candidates at the national level are right. In short, Hillary Clinton simply didn't belong not so much because she's an outsider (so is Trump) but because she vocally opposed what many in Appalachia view to be the region's lifeblood. Clinton went so far as to say: "We're going to put a lot of coal miners and coal companies out of business" when asked at a debate about the future of fossil fuels. Her answer, and the snark with which she delivered it, played well with her more urban supporters, but it fell flat in Appalachia. Rejecting coal, for many, meant rejecting Appalachian culture. Coal and outsider elitism are bound up as part of the same whole and it is impossible to consider one without considering the other. Combine Clinton's flippant remarks about coal miners with Trump's donning of a miner's hardhat at a campaign rally in West Virginia, and it isn't difficult to see why many in Appalachia put their chips on Trump's number.

Those who voted for Trump generally do not care what those outside the region think of their political leanings, and they aren't reading USA Today. They are, however, posting pictures of train-loads of coal on their Facebook walls, attributing the mining of those tons of coal directly to Trump, and they are sharing social media memes that criticize mainstream media outlets. The consumption and regurgitation of only those talking points that confirm their previously-held beliefs is not a practice unique to Appalachia. It happens all over the US. With Trump, however, many in Appalachia are motivated and perhaps even predisposed to support him by deeply embedded forces. To properly understand the Trump phenomenon in Appalachia, one must understand the region's political and economic power structures.

Perhaps more important than any other factor is the reality that Trump came to Appalachia and said, essentially, "I know that you exist and I'm going to help you." He walked onto a stage in Charleston, West Virginia, in May of 2016, donned a miner's hardhat, and told the coal miners in attendance that they should get ready to start mining more coal. Politics are often deeply personal in the hills of Appalachia, and the region has so long been ignored by most Americans that it is truly meaningful when a national political candidate not only visits the region but vows his support for their cause. They view every short ton of coal extracted from their region as further proof that Trump cares about them. Never mind that Trump's proposals are considered by outsiders to be disastrous for the region, or that coal has never been the sort of blessing for the region that coal boosters would have us believe. In Trump, many Appalachian people found an ally who they believed would fight for them.

For many, fighting for them does not mean the same thing as it means to the rest of America. Most people in Appalachia view the notion that those outside the region know what's best for them as yet another exercise in elitism. In fact, I myself hold this same view. It is offensive and insulting for many of us when those who know nothing about our region's culture or heritage, apart from perhaps what they've seen on reality TV or the in film Deliverance come to our mountains and try to tell us dumb hillbillies what we need. In Trump, Appalachian people found someone who listened to them and what they said they need – namely more coal mining – and pledged his support. While I disagree with the notion that more coal is what Appalachia needs to thrive economically, I cannot fault my neighbors for embracing a leader who took the time to acknowledge and value their own solutions to their problems. Instead, I am heartbroken that so many of my neighbors have yet again been led astray by a political leader preying on their vulnerability for personal and political gain.

For Appalachian people so accustomed to rough and dirty politics, their allegiance to Trump meant that they would support him come what may. They don't care about his alleged collusion with Russia, nor do they care that he is crude, crass, or short on intellect. Many are encouraged, not disheartened, by actions like the pardoning of former Maricopa County Sheriff Joe Arpaio. He's their guy, he says he looks after "his" people, and demonstrates it by doing things like pardoning Arpaio. In Appalachia, that still means something.

For those of us who study politics and power in Appalachia, Trump's popularity here is no surprise. In Appalachia, there's a long history of people supporting morally bankrupt and blatantly corrupt leaders. In fact, I would argue, based on my own scholarly work, that central Appalachia is the most politically corrupt place in the United States. Behaviors some of us view with distaste – vote buying, self-enrichment, and egomaniacal self-advancing policies – are just business as usual in Appalachia.

Consider that Appalachia is the region that still overwhelmingly supports villains like Don Blankenship. For those unfamiliar with the name, Blankenship was once the CEO of Massey Energy. He was convicted in 2015 of conspiring to violate federal law by ignoring safety violations at the company's Upper Big Branch Mine. As a result of Massey's actions, the court determined, 29 miners died in an explosion that could have been prevented.

In 2009, as many as 100,000 people turned out for a pro-coal rally on Labor Day sponsored by Blankenship and Massey. The rally featured conservative heroes Ted Nugent and Sean Hannity, among others. Clad in an American flag shirt, Blankenship declared that

"America's working families are under attack." Taxation and regulation, he argued, were the primary enemies of coal miners.

Of course, taxation and regulation are in fact the enemy of the coal barons, but Blankenship was able to successfully tie his own self-interest to that of rank and file coal miners. Despite what many view as behavior antagonistic to the best interest of workers and of the communities in which Massey operated, Blankenship made a rather compelling case that when Massey Energy was successful, so, too, was Appalachia. A rising financial tide for Blankenship's boat, in short, would be a rising tide for the region, too. So it is with Trump, it seems. Many blue-collar workers in Appalachia have connected their own futures to the success they hope to see Trump achieve.

While many of us view this false correlation as ridiculous at face value, the folks in Appalachia who flocked to Blankenship's 2009 rally did not view it that way. Blankenship himself boasted that he spent one million dollars to put on the event, and for many in attendance, it was an indication of Blankenship's deep commitment to his workers and to the region. When one considers Blankenship's efforts in comparison to Democrats like Clinton and President Obama who were pretty blatant about their disdain for the coal industry, it becomes pretty obvious who many in the region believe they should be supporting.

Mother Jones writer Tim Murphy writes that Blankenship "transformed West Virginia physically and politically." This is certainly true. He pumped millions of dollars into the coffers of Republican candidates for office. However, he was most certainly not the first coal baron to spend millions to buy political power in the coalfields. In fact, the region's history is full of corrupt by charismatic politicians who won the hearts and minds of the people even though their interests were largely selfish in nature.

It isn't just in industry that personalities like Blankenship find success and support. At a local level, politics in central Appalachia are often driven by oversized characters who thrive via a unique flavor of populism. Over and again, people in the region elect local political leaders who are blatantly corrupt and self-serving. What these corrupt local leaders usually share in common is a commitment to local people and an antagonistic approach to outsiders.

Knott County, Kentucky is a prime example of the way corruption is confronted differently in many parts of Appalachia than it is in most of the rest of the US. In 2006, Randy Thompson was appointed as Knott County Judge Executive, and was elected for a full term later that same year. Thompson, a prominent local business and media leader who owned a popular local radio station, was appointed to replace Donnie Newsome who resigned after being convicted of vote-buying. Newsome, it's worth noting, had run the county from prison for ten months before resigning.

Before Thompson could even complete his first full term in office, he, too, was convicted of vote-buying. In 2008, Thompson was found guilty of designing a scheme through which he was guaranteed political support and votes in exchange for paving private driveways with county materials and equipment. Thompson appealed.

In the meantime, having served his sentence, Newsome had his civil rights restored by the Governor of Kentucky and decided to try once again to become Judge Executive. In 2010, Newsome, previously convicted of vote-buying, briefly ran against Thompson, convicted of the same crime but still awaiting appeal. Newsome was defeated in the primary, but Thompson was reelected by the very voters the court determined he had cheated just a few years before. Thompson continued to serve as Judge Executive until he was forced by a judge to resign his office while serving his prison sentence. It is such a complicated web of corruption and elections that one almost needs a diagram to understand it.

There exists an extensive and often heartbreaking historical context to explain why Appalachia is different from the rest of the US both politically and economically. Much of the explanation traces back to a history of resource extraction and the takeover of the region by coal companies who bought local politicians and ruled with iron fists. To most outsiders who are unfamiliar with this historical context, Appalachia's brand of politics is baffling. However, when one considers that felons convicted of vote-buying can be reelected despite their crimes, and that Blankenship, a villain of cartoonish proportions, can attract 100,000 people to a Labor Day rally, it becomes easier to understand why Trump, who has no real operable solutions to the problems faced by most in Appalachia, was able to win in so many of the region's poorest counties.

The single worst mistake outsiders can make when attempting to interpret the actions of voters in Appalachia is to assume that they are simply too dumb to know any better. This is not the case. It is also not accurate to say that everyone in Appalachia supports Trump or Blankenship or corrupt local officials. It is worth noting that while a majority of voters in 95% of all counties in Appalachia voted for President Trump, that is not the same thing as 95% of Appalachia supporting him. Appalachia has a long history of resistance. However, the region has been so thoroughly defeated in so many ways over the course of multiple generations that those who resist often end up either giving up or moving away. Sometimes, they are defeated over and over until they just stop trying even if they can't afford to leave.

Appalachia is America's most neglected region. Despite efforts by the Appalachian Regional Commission and multitudes of federal elected officials, it is still a region in crisis. In many counties, the poverty rate tops thirty percent. In some, it tops forty percent. Those who spend any time in the region realize quickly that the people are in dire need of hope.

In Donald Trump, many in Appalachia found that hope. Because their region has functioned so far askew of American political norms for so long, they are able to overlook Trump's very evident flaws. After all, generations of corrupt Appalachian politicians have helped their constituents while simultaneously enriching themselves and maintaining power in dubious or illegal ways.

I would argue that many in Appalachia voted for Donald Trump in 2016 for the same reason that they voted for Randy Thompson in 2010. In both cases, they were supporting their guy. When Trump he said, over and over, that he was the only one who could fix the mess, he was echoing generations of Appalachian politicians. It is no wonder so many in Appalachia voted for him.

Until the Democratic Party first acknowledges that Appalachia does indeed exist and then offers the region some sort of tangible hope, those in the hills and hollers of West Virginia and eastern Kentucky will continue to vote for the candidate who puts on a hard hat and says "I recognize that you exist, and I'm going to help you."

Appalachia Needs a Reformation

October 31, 2017

As much as I think about (and complain about) the fundamentalist flavor of Christianity in which I was immersed as a kid, I'm surprised it took me so long to write about the topic on This Appalachia Life. As you might imagine, this essay was not particularly a hit with some members of my family. They probably went to the altar to pray for me after they read it, though in the eyes of the fundamentalists, criticizing their religion is likely the least of my sins.

Jesus wouldn't recognize the brand of fundamentalist Christianity being practiced today in a whole lot of Appalachian churches.

Growing up, I didn't know there was an alternative to the fundamentalist Southern Baptist Church. I spent Sundays and most Wednesday evenings inside little white churches that I would come to realize later were fully devoid of grace. I didn't really know what grace was until I was 31 years old. I heard plenty of sermons about it growing up, I sang about it, and I developed what I thought was a working understanding of it, but I realized one day that the definition of "grace" that had been beaten into my head for most of my life was wrong.

This week marks the 500th anniversary of the beginning of the Protestant Reformation. On October 31, 1517, Martin Luther marched up to the doors of the church in Wittenburg and nailed a document to the door. That document, titled the 95 Theses, outlined Luther's complaints against a Catholic Church that he viewed as corrupt and out of touch with the needs of its parishioners.

Though I am no Martin Luther, I think the time has come for those of us who understand the absence of grace in so many Appalachian churches to stand up and nail our complaints to the proverbial church door. Too many of our neighbors continue to suffer and be subjected to shame, humiliation, and rejection, all in the name of Christ. Knowing that, we cannot remain silent.

My own faith journey lead me at age 31 from the fundamentalist and closed-minded Southern Baptist Church to the Evangelical Lutheran Church in America (ELCA). In my hometown, there are over 100 Baptist churches, but only one Lutheran congregation. Given the ever-present nature of the Baptist Church, my long family history with fundamentalist Christianity, and the small number of Lutherans in Appalachia, my conversion was unlikely at best. However, the Spirit was indeed at work in my journey from scared and shameful Baptist to boldly-sinning Lutheran.

While most fundamentalist Baptists are quick to say that God is love, the sermons spouted from their pulpits on Sunday mornings are pretty solid evidence that they don't really believe this. Or, if they do, they believe God's love is reserved only for a select few who adhere, usually through a combination of fear and shame, to the preferred social views and norms of church leaders. Jesus loves you, but only if you don't drink beer, you aren't gay, your gender matches your genitals, you don't dance, you abstain from premarital sex, and, well, the list could go on for pages. Where's the grace in that?

I still remember the day I left the Baptist Church. It was Easter Sunday, and the local Director of Missions (sort of the Baptist equivalent of a Bishop, though their ecclesiastical structure doesn't recognize this title and they'd say it sounds way too Catholic) was preaching at the church where I grew up. I had recently rejoined that little church after having moved back to my hometown after a decade living away. I had been questioning my own faith for many years, and I thought that re-joining the church where I grew up might help me to finally grow some spiritual roots.

Church on Easter morning should be pretty straightforward, really. With a packed church, half of whom do not attend regularly and perhaps a quarter of whom have never darkened the doors of a church before, it would seem obvious what the message should be. However, this particular Easter morning, said the preacher, God had laid something special on his heart. He wanted to talk about alcohol and gay marriage.

He ranted and raved about the upcoming election. Our county was (finally – this was 2012, not 1921) voting on the sale of alcohol, and in North Carolina, Amendment One, which sought to prohibit same-sex marriage, was on the ballot. I was pretty pissed off that he chose Easter morning to get political, and the more I thought about it while he marched around and hollered and slung sweat, the angrier I got. Easter is about love and grace and resurrection. It isn't about some closed-minded asshole ranting and raving about politics and disguising it as the Gospel.

I gritted my teeth as the service wound down. I walked out of that church, the church two branches of my family started two generations before I was born, and I decided that I would probably never go back. By the time I got home, my anger had transformed into heartbreak. I grieved for all the people there that morning who had never been to church and those there who hadn't ever heard about Christ's love. What did they get from the service? God hates booze and homosexuals. Where's that in the Resurrection Sunday text, preacher?

Just as I had begun coming to terms with the faith that I had been questioning for the better part of a decade, I was knocked flat by a preacher spewing hate in the name of Christ. I could easily have lost my faith, and I probably should have, really. However, I decided that there must be something else, and oddly enough, I knew exactly where I'd turn to find it.

Just a few weeks before, I had met the pastor of the local Lutheran congregation. We frequented the same coffee shop, and a mutual friend introduced us. My first reaction, as a good Baptist, was to run away from this lady-pastor person, because of course, God don't call no women to preach. However, she and I sat down for a cup of coffee, and she challenged my faith in a way I didn't expect. I was armed for a theological argument in the way only those just finding or re-finding their faith might be. I was totally out of my league.

The first time we had a serious conversation about faith, she approached it in a way that disarmed me. Most of the pastors I had encountered in my life had one goal: conversion. For the Baptist preachers, just being Christian wasn't good enough. You had to be a Baptist. I expected the same from this Lutheran lady-pastor. I didn't get it. As we began talking about faith and conversions and such, I asked her what someone had to do in her faith tradition to "get saved." What, I asked, was the minimum amount of action one had to take to become a Christian? Sinner's prayer? Profession of faith? Baptism? Her response that day remains one of the most important moments in my own personal faith journey.

That day, Pastor Rosemary replied to my question not with an answer, but with another question. She asked me what anyone possibly could do, either through thought, word, or deed, to earn salvation. All the sudden, my Baptist vacation Bible school training kicked in, and I quoted a lot of scripture from Romans. There is none worthy, no not one, and so forth. Then my mind wandered to Ephesians. By grace through faith, and such. It hit me like a ton of bricks. There isn't a damned thing in the world I could think or do to earn salvation. It's a gift. Free for the taking. I'm not worthy of it, and that's the whole point. All the words I had been spouting off my whole life were thrown right back at me, debunking what I thought I believed, and the words came right out of my own mouth.

It took only seconds for me to realize that those formulaic "sinners' prayers" were garbage, not worth the cheap tracts on which they were printed. I realized that "asking Jesus into my heart" was an idiotic and meaningless concept invented by people who spouted "by grace, through faith," but insisted on those seeking to become Christian – to get "saved" – utter some magic words before being declared redeemed. Jesus did the work we aren't capable of doing. I wondered how I could have missed that all those years. It was that conversation, I suppose, that set me up to be so pissed off a few weeks later when that hateful preacher spouted ignorant political talking points, disguised as Gospel, from the pulpit of the little church I so loved.

The Sunday following Easter, I attended service at Pastor Rosemary's congregation, Shepherd of the Hills Lutheran Church, and I knew right away I had found my place. As I continued to think and pray and read, I realized that some part of me had been Lutheran my whole life. The theology resonated with me not just emotionally but intellectually. I finally understood that faith did not have to mean a rejection of science or reason or critical thinking.

As an unmarried man, I was essentially prohibited from many forms of service at the church where I grew up. I felt called to actively serve the church in a leadership role, but only married men were allowed to become deacons. I could teach Sunday School to the youth, but I wasn't interested in that. It isn't my gift. At Shepherd of the Hills, they welcomed me just as I was, and they put me right to work doing what I am called to do. Incidentally, when I met Betsy, the woman who would become my wife, they welcomed her, too, though she was not a prerequisite for my serving in leadership roles. I have taught Sunday School, assisted in worship, and served on Church Council, including as President.

The amazing people at our little Lutheran church have taught me what it means to be a Christian. It isn't about magic words or fear or shame or hell or even about heaven alone. It is about being Christ's hands on earth. It's about welcoming and loving everyone who comes through the door, just as they are, no matter their gender, socioeconomic status, religion, recovery status, sin history, or sexual orientation. My experiences at Shepherd of the Hills are what lead me to know, in the depths of my heart, that we must reform the Church in Appalachia.

When I decided to become a Lutheran, I began reading the works of Martin Luther. Perhaps the most meaningful part of Luther's work, for me, is his explanation of the human condition: simul justus et peccator. Simultaneously saint and sinner. Holy shit. Those words, when I first heard them, helped me to understand the world around me for the first time in my life. (They also helped me understand, by the way, that I could follow up the remarkable words of an historic pastor and Church leader with profanity.)

That "simultaneously saint and sinner" business is at the heart of why we must reform again. For far too long, the churches in Appalachia have focused too much on the sinner part while neglecting or ignoring the saint part. In the church where I grew up, one was one or the other, not both simultaneously. We were either in the favor of the preacher and church leaders, and consequently living within the will of God, or we were backsliding sinners who needed to march down the aisle to repent in front of everyone and confess our sins.

In my church experiences prior to the Lutheran Church, we were considered truly secure in our faith only when we were appearing to adhere to all the church's seemingly arbitrary and overly legalistic rules. Sure, most (though not all) Baptists purport to believe once-saved-always-saved, but the reality is that most will also question the salvation of individuals they deem to be living outside the church's social and cultural norms. I know at least a half a dozen people who have lived their lives so paralyzed by the fear of sin that they have been "saved" and baptized more than once. Again, where's the grace in that?

At the beginning of this essay, I said that I do not believe Jesus would recognize this brand of Christianity. When we begin to consider Jesus's ministry and his philosophy, it becomes apparent that many fundamentalist churches in Appalachia have become so obsessed with Paul's legalistic writings that they neglect the words of Christ himself.

If I were to characterize my experiences growing up in the fundamentalist Baptist Church, they would revolve around one word:

fear. I remember being twelve years old and going to church three times a week. My grandfather was the preacher. He was obsessed with Revelation, and he was convinced that the world would be ending soon with the Rapture. I would come to realize as an adult that "the rapture" is an utterly bullshit story invented in the 1830s by a crackpot amateur theologian named John Darby. However, at 12, I was scared shitless that the rapture would happen and I'd be left behind. I laid awake in bed every night convinced that I was about to bust the gates of hell wide open at any minute. Even after I said the magic words and got baptized, I was still convinced that some random sin was going to jeopardize my soul.

Today, when I think about Jesus, I think not about fear but about love. I think about service, sacrifice, and kindness. The Christ I have come to know is a warrior, but we are not the targets. Evil and injustice are Christ's targets. We are the beneficiaries. Christ's sacrifice is not reserved only for those who say the right magic words, or only those who belong to the right church, or only those who are straight, or only those who manage to avoid craft beer and bourbon their entire lives. No, Christ's sacrifice is for everyone. Like it or not, accept it or not, Christ died for you. Period.

Country Church
–Joshua Wilkey

Believers interject Amens and Alleluias while
the preacher dishes out hellfire in angry bursts,
as aged saints lift their wrinkled hands toward heaven.

Among the regulars, an unsaved face bound for hell,
so the preacher screams. Revelation, the rapture,
deathly battle, and a lake of fire are the threats.

The sermon runs out of gas, and the preacher
demands a song. On the piano, amateur fingers
fish for forgotten notes – Just As I Am.

Scared of hell, and scared as hell, believers
file to the front, kneel, pray. As they weep and
sob, the preacher asks won't you come...

More faithful followers file to the altar where
they kneel and pray, begging for a gift already
delivered, unaware of unearnable grace.

The music stops, the preacher prays, then offers
one last invitation to heaven. The unsaved face
stays put, as afraid of limelight as he is of hell.

In his heart, though, he thinks he'll go to heaven.

In 2013, the year after I became a Lutheran, the ELCA elected Elizabeth Eaton as the church's Presiding Bishop. Though I have never met her, words alone are not enough to express how much I appreciate her leadership of our church. Earlier this year, in an interview with the Chicago Sun-Times, Bp. Eaton said that if hell is a literal place, then it is empty. That's the thing about the resurrection. That's the thing that should have been made so abundantly clear on that Easter morning when I left the Baptist Church. Death has been defeated. Past tense. Christ's love was, and IS, powerful enough and sufficient enough. Present tense. Every Christian I know will say this is true. When will we start believing it?

If we believe in a resurrected Christ, we also have to understand that Christ is at work and at large in the world today. That's another thing I like about the ELCA. I'm normally skeptical of slogans, but the ELCA has a good one: "God's work, our hands." The first time I heard it, I had another "holy shit" moment. Turns out, I wasn't the only one to be struck by this idea. In the sixteenth century, Teresa of Avila wrote:

> Christ has no body but yours,
> No hands, no feet on earth but yours,
> Yours are the eyes with which he looks
> Compassion on this world,
> Yours are the feet with which he walks to do good,
> Yours are the hands, with which he blesses all the world.
> Yours are the hands, yours are the feet,
> Yours are the eyes, you are his body.
> Christ has no body now but yours,
> No hands, no feet on earth but yours,
> Yours are the eyes with which he looks
> compassion on this world.
> Christ has no body now on earth but yours.

If we are Christ's body, what are we doing about it? The idea of being Christ's body, I think, calls us to consider the proper role of the Church (capital "C" – as in, all Christians). What does it mean to be a Christian? Does it mean going to church every time the doors open, or does it call us to something more? So far as I know, Jesus sang zero Southern Gospel songs and attended zero covered dish dinners. Yet, that's sort of how we "do" church in Appalachia. There's the singing and the eating, and the fear and the shame.

Looking at Appalachian society, it is pretty clear that Jesus wouldn't be hanging out eating fried chicken and banana pudding with the preacher and his family. The churchy among us have become modern-day Pharisees. Judging by Jesus's actions in the Gospels, he would be at the local drug recover center working through a 12-step meeting with recovering addicts, telling them that they are not alone in their journey. He would be eating soup at the homeless shelter, comforting the hungry and chiding those of us who have plenty for not giving enough to those who have nothing. He'd be standing on the corner with the women who are selling their bodies to buy Oxycontin, telling them that they are worthy and that they are loved. He would be sitting on the bed of a nasty apartment beside an overdosing heroin addict, holding her hand as she ascends to a world where there is no more pain. He would also be a comforting presence to her children when they walk into the room to find her cold and lifeless body. He would be shivering beside freezing and hungry children in dilapidated trailers, and he would be sitting in local government meetings demanding clean water for those who have no access to it. He would be heartbroken as he watched corporate raiders destroy God's creation in the name of greed. He would be comforting those who can't find work, not blaming them for their plight or pledging to cut their SNAP and unemployment benefits.

In reality, we shouldn't write about these things as hypotheticals. Christ, resurrected and at large in the world, IS in these places. Jesus is looking to the outcast, the broken, and the shamed, and seeing not sinners, but saints. We should be, too.

However, these broken people are the ones we often shame the most. We shame them when they don't come to church, then when they do work up the courage to come, we shame them because of their sins and brokenness or because they don't wear the right clothes or because they have too many tattoos or piercings. We scare them into submission, threatening them with hell.

We tell them that if they remain broken, it must be because they are living outside of God's will. We tell them that if they would only love God enough, they'd be free from pain and suffering. Of course, this idea doesn't hold water theologically, but we focus so much on legalism that we blame the victims for their own brokenness rather than realizing that our own unwillingness to reach out to them in radical love and inclusion is itself a form of sinful brokenness.

When we go back and read the Gospels again and understand the way Jesus ministered and the people to whom he ministered, we realize that loving Christ and being Christ-like isn't about spouting hate from the pulpit. It isn't about finding some sort of obscure scriptural justification for our own social biases, and it isn't about controlling people with fear or uncertainty. Jesus sums up the Christian life in two commandments: love God, and love one another. When we understand that all humans, even the ones we don't like – even the assholes – are created in the image of God, how can we continue to justify spreading fear and hatred? How can we continue to act self-righteously when we see suffering all around us? How can we be content with our covered dish dinners and special Gospel singings when right outside our doors are people who are suffering and in dire need of love? How can we proclaim to be Christ's hands on earth when we realize that those who suffer the most often feel the most unwelcomed inside our churches?

If we are Christ's hands on earth, we are doing a pretty terrible job of it. That's why it is time for a new Reformation. It is time that we reach out to our neighbors not with shame but with love. It is time we start loving our neighbors who are suffering, whether they come to church or not. It's time to get our asses out of the pews and into the parts of our communities where we dare not tread. It is time we call out the hatemongering preachers who are paralyzing the poor and the broken with fear. It's time for an Appalachian Reformation. It's time we become a Church that Jesus might recognize when he returns.

Special thanks to Western Carolina University creative writing professor Pam Duncan. I wrote the poem above, "Country Church," in Pam's Introduction to Creative Writing class in 2013. I was a 32-year-old college sophomore struggling to find my place in the world while wrestling with the crisis in faith I describe in this essay. Pam empowered me to write about it even though I hadn't ever written about my emotions before. If there's anything good at all in me as a creative writer, it comes in large part from Pam's kind and gentle instruction. I am a better writer, and a better human, for having been her student. She was also kind enough to find this poem for me last year when I decided I wanted to use it for this essay but realized I had lost track of my copy.

The White-Trashification of the Opioid Epidemic

January 24, 2018

Unfortunately, the opioid epidemic seems to be here to stay for a while. As I watched the Trump Administration first ignore the problem apart from lip service, then offer some idiotic solutions, I began to think about how liberals aren't really getting it any more right than the conservatives. I attracted criticism from all sides for this essay, which leads me to believe that I might have gotten something right.

Drug addiction is an issue that continues to draw clear geographic, political, and class distinctions in the US.

Since the opioid epidemic began garnering national attention a few years ago, many of America's most prominent media outlets have devoted resources to covering it. Editors send their best writers into the most broken communities in rural America in an attempt to humanize the crisis that is stealing lives at an alarming rate. However, until we acknowledge the root causes of opioid abuse and addiction in rural communities, and admit our inherent biases toward the people who suffer most from this crisis, we stand little chance of ever solving it. More importantly, until Americans decide that poor, broken, and addicted people matter, nothing will change.

I have written previously about my own family's struggle with addiction and about the ways major pharmaceutical companies benefit from our heartbreak. Like most people who live in Appalachia, the opioid epidemic is personal for me rather than abstract. Members of my family have lost their lives and their livelihoods to opioids. However, no matter how many of us write our own stories, and no matter how many talented journalists come to our communities to write about the gravity of the opioid crisis, it seems impossible to push policy makers to actually do anything about it.

Members of Congress, both Republican and Democrat, give lip-service to the opioid crisis, but judging from their actions, it seems pretty clear that none of the elected officials in D.C. give two shits about a problem that primarily impacts rural white trash. Even those who represent the communities hardest-hit by the opioid epidemic offer little more than meaningless tough language and the standard "thoughts and prayers" rhetoric. Those thoughts and prayers aren't worth a damn to the people in rural America who are losing their family members to drugs, particularly when those offering said thoughts and prayers actually have the power to work toward meaningful solutions.

There are three important problems at play in the way Americans and American lawmakers are seemingly lethargic in their response to this crisis. First, while opioids ravage many rural communities, a few individuals and corporations are making billions by selling their poison to those who become hopelessly addicted to it. Second, there remains in the US a pervasive notion, despite reams of evidence to the contrary, that addition is simply the result of stupid people making poor choices. Finally, because the opioid epidemic largely targets poor and rural areas, there's less urgency on the part of urban elites to advocate for solutions. Taken together, these three problems are indications of why policymakers seem to have little interest in helping those whose lives and communities are being ruined by opioids.

I call these simultaneous processes the "white-trashification" of the opioid epidemic. For most Americans, the problem is a distant one. Those on the political right tend to attribute blame to the addicts, and those on the political left tend to think of it as a problem that affects primarily rural Trump voters who liberals perceive as voting against their own interests and therefore too ignorant (or hateful or racist) to care about. In both instances, the victims are perceived as white trash whose lives and stories, let's be honest, are not always important to Americans. As Nancy Isenberg's book *White Trash: The 400-Year Untold History of Class in America* indicates, those on the lower end of the socioeconomic spectrum have existed outside the mainstream of American life for generations. So long as Americans can continue to "other" those suffering from the opioid epidemic, in the same way they've always "othered" white trash, there exists little hope of relief.

I realize that "white trash" is a loaded and caustic term. Last summer, I wrote an essay titled "Blessed are the White Trash," and since the publication of that essay, I get emails regularly from folks who are upset about my use of the term. I understand the raw emotion attached to that term more than most people. I grew up white trash. When I was in school, other kids picked on me because of my white trash status. Largely because I grew up in this environment, I developed imposter syndrome. I let other people convince me for much of my life that, because I came from poverty, I would never be as good as everyone else. I continue to use "white trash" because I know firsthand what a powerful term it is. I want to take ownership of it, turn it around, and show those who continue to use it in a hurtful manner just how hateful and despicable a concept it is. I believe that words mean things, and I continue to use these words because the phrase "white trash" is more meaningful and powerful than any euphemism for the concept could ever be. Because of the power of this term, and the psychological baggage that comes with it, I believe it is important for us to explore the white-trashification of things like the opioid epidemic.

The first part of this white-trashification process involves the influence and power of the corporations that manufacture and distribute opioids. I have a fundamental mistrust of large corporations in part because I have devoted my career to studying the problematic nature of power structures in global history. Primarily because of the role of prescription drug manufacturers in the opioid epidemic, I have a hard time conceptualizing drug companies as benevolent providers of miracle cures. Sometimes, they do important work. Other times, though, they are simply predators, preying on sick and broken people for the sake of profit. Purdue Pharma, in particular, engages in a brand of evil that should shock our sensibilities. Their popular painkiller Oxycontin has caused more heartbreak and death than perhaps any legal drug in American history, and Purdue has been shamefully responsible for getting people hooked on the drug.

Purdue and other pharmaceutical corporations have lawmakers on their side. They pay their political dues, and the result is that these politicians continue to avoid cracking down on Purdue for poisoning communities and killing Americans with their products. Often, Purdue gives money to lawmakers whose own constituents are dying from Oxycontin. For example, in the 2016 election cycle, Purdue wrote a check for $10,000 to one of my senators, Richard Burr. Thousands of Burr's constituents in rural North Carolina have died from Oxycontin, but addicts lack political clout. Realities like this lead me to have little hope that lawmakers will crack down on the pharmaceutical companies who are responsible for fueling the opioid epidemic with deadly addictive products and aggressive marketing practices.

The second part of the white-trashification process involves the unfortunate and widespread blaming of the victims whose lives are destroyed by opioids. Every time I write about the opioid crisis, people leave comments on my social media posts blaming addicts for their addictions. These comments infuriate me, because I can't help but think that they usually come from people who have never been willing to understand the world as addicts experience it. They come from a place of mean-spirited disregard for human suffering. These people believe that addiction is a moral failing, not a disease. These people are wrong. As David Sheff demonstrates in his book *Clean: Overcoming Addiction and Ending America's Greatest Tragedy*, science should be at the heart of how we treat addiction in the U.S., and viewing addiction as a moral failing rather than as a disease defies the science of addiction and recovery.

Because opioid addiction disproportionally targets the rural poor, it is even easier to dismiss these suffering humans as white trash and attribute their woes to their own stupid choices. This line of thinking offensive and out of touch with scientific fact, and it also conveniently ignores the fact that most of the individuals who are addicted to opioids first got the drugs from medical professionals who prescribed them legally. This reality reveals a troubling blind spot in the way healthcare professionals treat pain. While there certainly exists a genuine need to prescribe opioid painkillers, we must decide where to draw the line between treating legitimate pain and exposing individuals in pain to dangerously addictive drugs. Particularly since opioid manufacturers were often dishonest with healthcare providers about the addictive nature of their drugs, it is long past time for hard and serious conversations about limits on these powerful drugs.

The final part of the white-trashification of the opioid epidemic combines this victim-blaming mentality with the reality that most victims of the opioid epidemic live in impoverished rural areas, isolated from urban centers. While opioids are an equal-opportunity poison, those in urban areas and those from households of elevated socioeconomic status have plenty of financial and healthcare resources to treat addiction. Those who live in rural communities lack both the healthcare infrastructure to treat addiction and the financial resources to pay for recovery treatment. When those who live in urban areas see family members and others in their communities struggling with opioid addiction, they often also see the plethora of resources available to addicts from affluent families or locales. It is easy to assume, then, that those in rural areas might also have access to readily-available treatment. This is not the case.

This chasm between rural and urban Americans also reveals a widening divide in political ideologies between those in urban areas and those who live in rural communities. Stereotypically, urban areas are blue and rural areas are red. The electoral map from the 2016 election indicates that this is generally the case in recent years. Accordingly, an increasingly bitter view of urban liberals toward rural conservatives can potentially influence the way those in urban areas view those who suffer most from the opioid epidemic. Even when top-notch media outlets send reporters to rural communities to personalize and humanize the tragedy, it is easy for left-leaning urbanites to write those struggling with opioid addiction off as Trump supporters, and, therefore, intellectually and culturally unequal. As we continue to struggle in the U.S. with polarized political views, it becomes even less likely that left-leaning urban-dwellers will develop enough sympathy for right-leaning rural folks to advocate aggressively on their behalf. That being the case, then, the only advocates left for many conservative rural Americans, apart from themselves, are their elected representatives, who are almost exclusively Republicans bought and paid for by big pharma.

Though I have little faith that urban Democrats and rural Republicans will ever understand their shared values, I believe one of the keys to addressing the opioid epidemic is for all Americans understand the nefarious nature of those who perpetuate the cycle of addiction, even when those responsible wear expensive suits or white coats. The problem is perpetuated by greedy corporations and by unethical doctors who run strip-mall pain clinics. This should piss Democrats off regardless of who the victims are. However, the political left has shown very little regard for rural America in recent years. This blind spot, incidentally, is one of the leading factors in Donald Trump's electoral success. I also hold little faith that rural Republicans will ever understand that the people they send to D.C. to represent them actually represent the interests of wealthy donors who see rural Americans not as people to serve but as profit centers to exploit. To be elected, GOP members of Congress need only go to their districts, shout about how the liberals want to take away guns and murder babies moments before their birth, and ride the resulting wave of anger back to election. Similarly, urban Democrats need only yell about increasing inequality (while simultaneously doing nothing about it) and accuse Republicans of trying to rob people of healthcare. It is almost never necessary for either group to acknowledge the sufferings of those of different political leanings.

Despite these political impasses that inject the American political process with the a sort of stasis that guarantees no progress, some stark realities remain. In 2016, even though the prescribing rate of opioids had fallen from 2012 record highs, there were as many opioid prescriptions as residents in a full twenty-five percent of all U.S. counties. In some counties, there were enough opioid prescriptions for each person to have four prescriptions. Common sense should dictate that even in the sickest counties there should not be such a saturation of opioid painkillers. Any reasonable person should look at those statistics and know that something is broken. Yet, despite these stunning statistics and dire warnings from the Centers for Disease Control and Prevention, very little tangible action is being taken by the federal lawmakers who have the power to fix this mess. The opioid epidemic has become nothing more than another political talking point meant to fool voters into thinking that elected officials care about suffering humans.

As I said at the outset of this essay, until Americans decide that poor, broken, and addicted people matter, nothing will change. Recently, we witnessed the aggressive promotion of tax cuts that disproportionately benefits profitable corporations and the wealthy while Congress continued to refuse to provide funding for the Children's Health Insurance Program. If one is to interpret the political actions of the elected elites in the U.S. as an indication of which humans matter and which do not, then regardless of which party is in power, it becomes evident rather quickly that poor people simply do not matter. Therefore, Americans will continue to watch their neighbors die in record numbers and write them off either as addicts who should have made better choices or as rural white trash who should make better choices at the ballot box.

Today, on Lockdown, I Didn't Miss My Gun

February 28, 2018

I often intend to write pieces that are timely to current events, but given my schedule and the precious little time I find to write most weeks, I tend to lag so far behind that what I want to write is rarely relevant by the time I get around to writing it. However, after my first experience with a lockdown at work and in the wake of the Parkland, FL school shooting, I knew I had to write about guns.

Earlier today, as I sat in a darkened college classroom with my students, doors locked and shades closed for fear that an active shooter might be at large on our campus, I knew that the current dialogue surrounding school shootings would never be impersonal or distant for me again.

For fifty-nine of the longest minutes of my life, surrounded by scared but resilient students, I wondered what was happening down the hall, across the quad, and across campus. For almost half of those minutes, I thought there was a chance that a shooter might at any minute violate the sanctity of my own classroom.

Every time there has been a mass shooting in the past couple of years, I have felt compelled to write about it, but every time, I watch the national conversation devolve into angry and non-productive partisan shouting matches. Even the hateful talking point parroting fades away after a week or so, and we never approach anything resembling a rational debate about why we are the only developed nation where children are murdered at school by white men wielding semi-automatic weapons. There seems to be little appetite for middle ground in the debate about guns and mass shootings.

For me, things are different after today. The potential for a mass shooting has come to my campus and to my classroom. I have stared it in the face. I have watched my students struggle to come to terms with it. I'm done being silent about it.

Particularly given the polarized nature of discussions about gun control, I have largely avoided writing about this topic because, in many ways, I find myself occupying a middle ground. Though my own personal positions on gun control have shifted over time, I understand arguments from both sides even when I don't always agree.

I grew up around guns. I learned to shoot when I was young. I got my first gun when I was still a pre-teen, though I was allowed to use it only under very close supervision. I was 12 years old the first time I used a high-powered rifle to take a deer. As an adult, I got a concealed carry permit, and when I lived in Eastern Kentucky, I carried a concealed handgun most everywhere I went, because many of my travels were to unsafe places. I shot competitively for a while, and when I carried a concealed handgun regularly, I shot 150-200 rounds a week to stay in practice. I kept a 12-gauge shotgun by my bed, a .38 revolver in my nightstand, and an AR-15 in the closet. Looking back, I'm not sure what I was afraid of, but whatever it was, I was ready for it.

At age 31, when I transitioned from small business owner to first-time college student, I owned a large number of firearms, and they were worth thousands of dollars. By that point, however, I had become wary of gun culture. I enjoyed shooting sports and hunting, and believed strongly in my right to carry a weapon and defend myself. However, I had begun to notice just how insane the gun industry's rhetoric was becoming.

Their goal, pretty clearly, wasn't to defend freedom, whatever that means. Their goal was to sell more guns and more gun stuff. The NRA and gun manufacturers were counting on gun people to bolster their bottom lines. Cloaked in grandiose patriotism and prodded to action by celebrity spokespeople, many gun owners began to think that it was their God-ordained duty to buy as many guns as they could afford. I saw it happening, and it disgusted me. What disgusted me more were the insane conspiracy theories that circulated among the gun rights crowd. Birtherism and false flag operations and illegal terrorist immigrants the like were, in many ways, just more encouragement for gun people to buy more guns. I finally decided that I was done buying into this culture.

When I left Kentucky in 2010 to return to my hometown in North Carolina, I sold most of my guns. I no longer felt a need to carry a concealed weapon, because I didn't feel unsafe anymore. Getting away from the bombastic rhetoric of gun culture did wonders for my ability to live without fear. I still slept with a Glock under my pillow for a while, but eventually, like most of my other guns, I sold it for tuition money. These days, the only guns we have at home are a WWI-era rifle and a couple of .22 caliber varmint-guns, which are standard on most any rural homestead like ours. In our neighborhood, I'm substantially more concerned about coyotes and copperheads than about criminals or terrorists, so we are armed accordingly.

In the days following the Parkland school shooting, as politicians began pushing to arm teachers, I started to think about my own position on the issue given that I am a college professor who spends hours every day inside classrooms. In general, I am opposed to guns on campus, particularly when they are carried by students. The notion of a half a dozen guns flying out of waistbands and backpacks when a shooter bursts into the classroom does not make me comfortable, especially since I would be standing between those gun and said shooter and lots of testosterone and raw emotion would be involved. I am not confident that arming teachers would make a bit of difference, either. Carrying concealed, especially in the sort of professional attire worn by educators, does not lend itself to fast drawing. If I were carrying a small handgun in an ankle holster, as I have many days in my life, there's no way I could draw it, take aim, and discharge it at a shooter rushing into my classroom armed with an AR-15 before being mown down by the shooter's bullets. As someone who has carried concealed weapons regularly at times in my life, I understand the logistical limitations. Those who are proposing concealed carry for teachers have perhaps not thought it through.

One of the more ridiculous arguments comes from Wayne LaPierre, head of the NRA. As recently as this week, he said that the only way to stop a bad guy with a gun is for good guys to have guns. First and foremost, I refuse to start the conversation at "bad guy with a gun" when there are plenty of steps that we must take to ensure that bad guys do not in fact get guns. It is not inevitable that bad people end up with guns, and there's plenty of evidence to back this up if we look beyond our own borders. The more problematic part of this idea, however, is that it assumes that those who are bad are always bad, and those who are good are always good. As Martin Luther so poignantly noted, we are simul justus et peccator. Simultaneously saint and sinner. We are all both good and bad. A good guy with a gun is a good guy until, well, he isn't. Guns do not evaporate when those wielding them make fleeting or permanent transitions from good to bad. Therein lies the rub. Yesterday, he was a good guy. Today, he's a bad guy. He has the same gun in both circumstances.

It is also problematic to argue, as President Trump has, that potential mass shooters would be dissuaded by the fact that some teachers would be packing heat. Most perpetrators of mass killings carry out their crimes not because it's convenient, but because they are determined to kill even if it means losing their own lives. Often, these mass shooters take their own lives when they are done killing, and they know that they are likely to be killed by those who respond to their shootings. The 2009 Fort Hood shooter carried out his crime on a military base, where literally almost every person he encountered was trained in the use of firearms. He didn't do it because it was easy or because he thought there would be little risk. To argue that the potential to encounter armed resistance would keep these deranged individuals from carrying out mass shootings is to indicate a complete lack of awareness about the realities of these crimes and the monsters who commit them.

As I said at the outset of this essay, there is very little middle ground in national debates about guns. Conservatives remain convinced that liberals are trying to take away their guns. Liberals continue to make absurd claims about scary-sounding phrases like "assault weapon" and "semi-automatic gun" without even knowing what these phrases really mean. The tin-foil-hat brigade, led by nuts like Alex Jones, is screaming about Nancy Pelosi coming to get our guns, while the angriest and most uninformed voices on the left are trying to put my semi-automatic .22 squirrel rifle into the same category as an AR-15.

I am encouraged this week by attempts at bipartisanship. Even President Trump has staked out some positions that run counter to the NRA, though I'm not convinced he will stick with them. There are so many common-sense initiatives that could be implemented, all of which have widespread support among Americans, and none of which would infringe on Second Amendment rights. I tend to be a jaded observer, but at a time like this, I need to hope that the unhinged lunatics at the NRA can be overcome by common sense.

It's those NRA folks like Wayne LaPierre, incidentally, who are at the heart of this problem. I was once a proud NRA member. I grew up reading *American Rifleman* when I could get my hands on copies of it. I used to love to go fox hunting with my grandfather because the hunting cabins we would stay in were always stocked with copies of *American Rifleman*, the official magazine of the NRA. Back then, it was full of good stories about guns, hunting, and the great outdoors. However, by the time I reached adulthood, the magazine had become nothing but a tool with which the NRA scared its members into action. Somewhere along the way, there was a shift, and along with this shift was the genesis of a toxic gun culture.

When I was a kid, I'd sometimes hang around my uncle's gun shop. I loved the smell of gun oil almost as much as I loved the stories the men who hung out there would tell. It was always a positive experience for me in a childhood that sometimes lacked positive moments. Seldom was there any talk about politics. Two decades later, as an adult and small business owner with extra money to afford a gun or three, I encountered a much different culture at the various gunshops I frequented. Gone were most of the fun hunting and shooting stories. In their place were rabid Republican political talking points, frenzied talk about liberals coming to take away our guns, and a potent combination of fear and consumerism that drove customers to buy as many guns as they could afford in anticipation of some gun rights doomsday event.

The other new element in the gunshops of my adulthood: AR-15 rifles. Sure, they existed when I was a kid, but I didn't know anyone who had one. These days, I don't know many gun people who don't have one. I won't pretend that I don't enjoy shooting AR-15s. I have owned a number of them, and they are indeed fun to shoot. However, they were designed for a single purpose: to kill humans. They are weapons of war. Period. While some will argue that they are useful for hunting, most gun people know better. Whether it's taking large game like deer or eliminating invasive varmints like coyote, there are better-equipped rifles for these tasks. I might buy the argument that the AR-15 is an effective means of home defense, but I'll take a pump-action 12-gauge shotgun with 00 buckshot at my bedside any day over an AR-15.

One of the more striking features of the AR-15 is that 30-round magazines are standard. Because it is semi-automatic, the AR-15 will shoot as fast as one can pull the trigger. Equipped with a bump stock device, it shoots even faster. These high-capacity magazines are a feature designed for the weapon's primary mission: to kill people. If we cannot agree that these high-capacity magazines should be banned, then we must come to terms with the reality that they make it possible to slaughter large numbers of people in short amounts of time. Are we so obsessed with our alleged freedom to own high-capacity magazines for weapons designed to slaughter humans that we are willing to continue to see children gunned down with these weapons at school?

Wrapped in red, white, and blue, and whipped into an angry frenzy by LaPierre's NRA, today's gun culture is toxic. It is steeped in consumerism, driven by paranoia, and wholly out of touch with what was once good and laudable and wholesome about communities centered around the outdoors and shooting sports. The terrifying reality is that most mass shooters -- perhaps most notably the Charleston shooter Dylann Roof -- are steeped in this new and toxic gun culture. Their social media feeds and those who know them confirm this reality. While this toxic gun culture alone might not drive mass shooters to murder, it is an unavoidable part of the problem.

As we continue to grapple with what it looks like to debate gun control and mass killings, we have to debate in good faith. At this point, the NRA cannot do so. In his recent speech to CPAC, LaPierre demonstrated that he is completely detached from reality. Peddling conspiracy theories and demonizing those who seek in good faith to endeavor to solve hard problems, LaPierre indicated his stedfast refusal to engage in constructive dialogue about guns. Therefore, the NRA should not have a seat at the table. When their only goal is obstruction, they are not worthy of sitting at the same table as men and women who are passionate about reaching across the aisle to solve these heartbreaking problems.

In the days leading up to today, as politicians and talking heads debated guns in classrooms, I wondered, despite my own theoretical opposition to more guns on campus, if I would regret not being armed if a shooter burst into my classroom. I wondered if, when evil was in close proximity and on the move, I might yearn for the weight and the reassuring comfort of a Glock 23 tucked into a leather holster inside the waistband of my pants.

Today, as my students and I sat there in that dark classroom, knowing that there could be a shooter nearby, I thought about my own experiences with guns, and about the times in my life I had been grateful to be carrying a concealed handgun. I thought of the time I was accosted on the sidewalk of the town where I lived in Kentucky by a meth addict who threatened to hurt me if I didn't give him my wallet. When I gently brushed my suit jacket back to expose the shoulder holster and .45 underneath, he apologized and moved on. I thought back to a few days ago when I first wondered if I would wish for a gun in the face of danger on campus.

As I thought about it, actively aware that a shooter could be on the way down the hall, I had no regret that there wasn't a gun inside my waistband or in my pocket or in a holster on my ankle. In that moment, sitting ten feet from the door of my classroom, between an imaginary shooter and 21 students I adore, I decided that if the door flew open and a shooter came through, I would rush toward the door and do my damnedest to stop him. In ten feet, I couldn't get off a shot if I were carrying a concealed handgun, but I could run at him and block his gun spray and perhaps disarm him.

In that moment, I rejected the false dichotomy that poisons our current gun debate. I knew, in amazing clarity, that there was a middle way between cowering helplessly in fear and carrying a gun in macabre anticipation of a school shooting that might never happen. Today, when we were all afraid that the proverbial wolf had found his way to our door, I knew that if I died defending my classroom, I would be yet another symbol of a society too polarized and self-absorbed to confront gun violence with good faith and a steadfast commitment to loving our neighbors more than our political ideologies or our guns. I believe we are better than that, though our lack of ability to engage one another in these discussions would seem to indicate otherwise.

I Don't Write About Crafts

If you really want to piss me off, fill out the contact form on my website to ask me why I don't write more about the "charming" parts of Appalachia.

I probably won't reply, but if I did, you wouldn't like it very much. I usually don't reply to these queries because it's hard to do so without using profanity, and it isn't very hospitable to throw profanity at the people who read your writing.

Nevertheless, there's a reason I don't write about the fluffy parts of Appalachian history. This essay is a long-overdue response to the dozens of emails I have gotten from folks asking me to write more about the version of Appalachian culture and history they expect to read rather than the version that actually exists.

The charming stereotypical version of Appalachian history goes something like this: Long ago, hard-working and fiercely independent Scots Irish settlers made their way across the ocean and found these noble mountains. Here, they carved out homesteads and communities where they grew and produced all they needed. They relied on the bounty of the land. They even learned how to use local plants and animal products by consulting with their new friends the Indians! In particular, they made use of the corn that grows so abundantly here. Their kids played with cornshuck dolls, they made brooms from corn, and they even made their own liquor from fermented corn mash! Gosh, those noble outlaws who made the moonshine liquor even invented a new sport called NASCAR!

I can't type that version out without rolling my eyes and getting a little sick, but the truth is, if I were to stop any of the out-of-state folks staying in the AirBnB rentals up the holler from our house and ask them to describe traditional Appalachian culture, they'd probably give me some version of this overly romanticized garbage. Of course, there's a chance they might have seen *Deliverance* or *Justified*, so they might also talk about meth and Oxycontin and incest, but these are tourists who paid good money to come here on vacation, so they expect to see and hear about the charming parts. These are the same sorts of folks, I assume, who email me when they get home to complain that I don't write about fucking cornshuck dolls.

If they knew that just up the road from their charming three bedroom rental cabin was a trailer with an odd assortment of genuine Appalachian folks who are home usually only when they aren't serving a stretch at the county jail for trafficking drugs, they might realize that the charming version of Appalachia they've been sold by crafty tourism promoters is, in large part, a crock of shit.

This problem of reality versus tourist expectation is at the heart of why I don't write fluffy Appalachian history. There really isn't any getting around the fact that tourism has resulted in a distorted view Appalachian identity. When the railroads made their way into Appalachia in the 1880s and 1890s, the region began to attract tourists almost immediately. Flatlanders from South Carolina, Virginia, and Georgia sought out cooler mountain climates, and resort towns sprang up all across the mountains. The Local Color Writers movement exposed places like Appalachia to the rest of the US, which spurred even more people to come visit.

These visitors had occasion to interact with locals, and the result was the birth of myriad stereotypes. Both the noble mountaineer and the lazy hillbilly were born in this era. Some tourists decided that Appalachian people were a sort of snapshot of a previous era. They were, perhaps, just the same in the 1890s as their ancestors were when they first laid eyes on the mountains. Others saw opportunity and set out to dupe the noble mountaineers out of land, resources, and labor. This is where we find the divergence that set the region up for generations of exploitation and poverty.

Not all those who visited Appalachia in the late 1800s came only for respite and cool mountain air. Many came for opportunity. Coal had been discovered in Central Appalachia, and much of the region was covered with valuable and highly marketable timber. In short order, these outsiders began engaging in land speculation and unscrupulous acquisition of mineral and timber rights. It was at this point that Appalachia became a rich land with poor people.

For me, it is impossible to tell the story of Appalachia without telling this part. The systematic exploitation of Appalachia is not just something unfortunate that happened. It is the cornerstone of Appalachian history. Without this exploitation or the development of a robust extraction economy, Appalachia would look completely different today. That's why I can't just focus on the fluffy stuff. No matter how cool or interesting or quaint or beautiful it is, the more innocent parts of Appalachian history – foodways, dialect, crafts, homesteading – cannot exist in a vacuum, and they cannot be understood except as part of a larger history.

It just feels dirty to me to obsess over the more pleasant parts of the region's history while glossing over or completely ignoring the heartbreaking parts. Cornshuck dolls and quilts are poor compensation for intergenerational poverty, and no matter how many millions of tourists we attract by focusing on these things, we will still never achieve the potential the region's people would have been capable of had they not fallen victim to robber barons and carpetbaggers who took and took without ever bothering to invest in local communities in meaningful ways. No matter how proud we are of the ways we think our forebears survived in these mountains, we can't escape the reality that the descendants of many from outside the region were enriched at the expense of our ancestors. It's not a pretty story, but it is one that has to be told.

Also absent from the fluffier version of Appalachian history is the way absentee resource companies used hired gun thugs to bust up the unions seeking to bring about safer working conditions and more stable lives for coal and timber workers. While those who want to know about Appalachian music and crafts and cornbread are busy seeking out the best place to eat pancakes or experience authentic Appalachian culture, whatever that means, they often fail to notice the decided lack of a robust middle class in many parts of the region. They are so engrossed in making cornshuck dolls at Dollywood that they fail to recognize the tragedy in a culture so often impoverished that they made toys for their kids out of what urban yuppies throw into the compost bin.

As for me, I refuse to give in and write about the hardscrabble parts of my own history as if it's somehow quaint or noble. It isn't. It's the result of systematic forces that have, for generations, conspired to extract as many resources from our region as possible while reinvesting as little as possible.

I have a tremendous amount of respect for the generations of folks who survived in these mountains. They were ingenious. They scraped out livings in places where others couldn't, and they did so often while outside actors were actively trying to exploit them. The people of Appalachia are not innocent victims, but, rather, people who exhibited individual agency in the face of seemingly insurmountable odds. This, to me, is worthy of celebration. I'm just not sure how I feel about visitors celebrating the innovative survival skills of Appalachian folks when those very visitors, or more likely their grandparents and great-grandparents, benefitted from the systems that pillaged the region. There's an odd perversion in this. It's as if you kicked a dog then later celebrated its skittishness.

I realize that my line of argument seems isolationist. Perhaps I'm exhibiting some of the clannishness that Appalachian folks are alleged to be prone to. However, as we consider the contemporary condition of reality, we must recognize that the region is as it is because of historical forces that made it this way. Those who are truly interested in the history of Appalachia should make an effort to look past the kitschy parts of the region and understand the broader economic and political forces that conspired to create an environment in which Appalachian people were forced to find innovative ways to survive. However, no one wants to pay money to visit a pretty place only to learn that its people have remained poor largely because shitty American capitalists conspired to pillage the region at the expense of its inhabitants.

 While it isn't for me, there are some people and some institutions who do a good job at preserving the parts of Appalachian history so many tourists want to see. In my professional career as an historian, I have pushed to be sure that museums and living history sites tell a robust version of Appalachian history. I want visitors to know not only that Appalachian people made toys out of crop waste and used every part of a hog except the oink but that they did so out of necessity. I also want them to know that while the people of Appalachia were struggling to survive, outsiders were making billions off the resources extracted from Appalachia.

 In an ideal world, Appalachia would be a rich land with rich people, but throughout the whole of human history is has been more likely that resource-rich lands were inhabited by poor people. Some scholars call the "resource curse." Perhaps the version of Appalachian culture that tourists pay good money to hear about is a product of that resource curse. The same forces that brought us create cornshuck dolls also pushed our region toward the opioid epidemic, intergenerational poverty, and, in many cases, environmental catastrophe. All these things are part of the same storyline, and it's rarely sunshine and rainbows.

 I yearn for a time when these stories will be treated as a coherent narrative. I wish people could simultaneously hear about Appalachian innovation and the soul-crushing poverty that spurred it. However, nobody wants to pay money to hear about the messy parts, and I'm not interested in telling only half of the story.

JOSHUA WILKEY

ABOUT THE AUTHOR

A lifelong resident of Appalachia, Joshua Wilkey lives in rural western North Carolina. An historian, educator, and part-time poultry farmer, he and his wife Betsy live on a little homestead where they raise organic vegetables and herd an array of chickens, guinea fowl, ducks, and turkeys.

Made in the USA
Columbia, SC
30 April 2019